On Going to Hell

On Going to Hell

Daniel Schifeling

First Printing, 2026

Published by Santos Books, LLC

ISBN: 979-8-9936553-6-9

CONTENTS

For Barbara, the love of my life,
and for our family.

This is a book about going to hell.

If you are like me, ending up in hell is usually something you wish on *others* during your worst moments. If someone makes me mad enough, I have been known to wish that *they* will go to hell in revenge for whatever they did to aggravate *me*. It's small-minded, I know. But I take some comfort in the truth that I have no real power to send them anywhere. I get a moment of comic relief as I imagine their panic at roasting in the eternal flames, and then I forget about it and move on. Imagining them in hell helps me avoid stewing about what happened. It's kind of a stress reliever, although I confess it doesn't pass muster and please God.

The prospect of hell is more than a stress reliever, however. As I grow older – I'm 79 – I am reflecting more seriously on what my life will amount to in God's eyes. How have I done as a person and as a pastor? What have I made of the tremendous gifts God's Spirit has bestowed on me? What will be the legacy I leave on earth, and what will I experience on a day of reckoning with the One who created me? These are truly serious questions to me right now. Indeed, they are questions I believe we all should ponder.

Which brings me to the reason I am writing this book. Hell is a place most Christians believe in. (Gallup polls confirm this.) The certainty of God's judgment and the possibility that God, through Jesus, will send us to hell is a big point of emphasis in Jesus' teachings and is featured in other parts of the New Testament. As we all agree, hell is not the final destination anyone wants.

The thing about hell, however, is that we pretty much believe that it is a place *others* are going to. I remember being about eight years old when my neighborhood friend remarked out of the blue that I was damned. "You know you're going to hell when you die, don't you?" he said. I was startled. "No," I said. "Well, you are," he said. "The priest at my school told me that all Protestants are going to hell." I was a Protestant. I had some idea what hell meant. I didn't really think my everyday life was bad enough to deserve being sent there. "I don't think that's right," I said. "I don't think it's true." But at the dinner table that night, I told my parents what my friend had said. They reassured me that Protestants are also good people, along with Roman Catholics, but it stuck in my head. Seriously confronting someone with the possibility that they are headed to hell is no small thing.

Yet, I am writing to ask millions of Trump supporters, including his Christian supporters, to consider the real possibility that their behavior in supporting him, and the condition of their souls that results from their support, is so bad that it has them headed to hell... and that if they do not repent and change their hearts and minds and behavior, they may end up in an eternal state of hell. At least, that is what the Bible says, not just once or twice, but over and over again.

Reading this, you may feel outrage. What am I, a progressive Christian minister, doing by suggesting that some evangelical Christians are risking damnation? My guess is that you are used to being told by your pastors that evangelicals are the ones who are saved. After all, you have accepted Jesus Christ as your Lord and Savior. You believe that Jesus died for your sins and won you a place in heaven. You think salvation is not a matter of works, but of faith. Since you believe you are in. At some point, you may have prayed the Jesus prayer, accepting Jesus as your personal Lord and Savior, and by doing that, you were told that you were guaranteed to go to heaven. You may also have been told that folks like me, who you suspect have not accepted Jesus as my personal savior, are the ones who are going to hell.

So, if you are a Trump supporter, you are likely telling *me* to go to hell right now! And I understand your anger and even scorn. I want to assure you, however, that I am writing this book out of kind motives. I do *not* want you to go to hell! I will take no satisfaction if you refuse to listen to a word I say. As a minister of Jesus Christ, I want you to thrive.

I simply believe that if you support so many unloving things and then believe that God is cheering you on, you have wandered from the narrow path that leads to salvation and are out on the broad and easy path that leads to destruction.

How can we agree on what is the right way to live and to be saved from the temptations of this world? If you are an evangelical Christian, then I think I can assume that you believe in the Bible. In fact, I think you believe that the Bible is the inerrant word of God, so that if the Bible says something, then it must be true. Even more, I think you respect the Bible as giving us explicit instructions from God on how to live. The Bible is "the Good Book". It will never steer us wrong. So, let's agree that in this conversation about judgment and hell – and who will end up in hell – that the Bible will be our standard. If we disagree, we will look to the Bible to tell us who is right. Regarding the Bible, I will generally use the New Living Translation (NLT). I will cite it the first time I quote from the Bible as a reminder, but after that, I will only note the version if it is not the NLT.

One more thing I need to add about the Bible. For as long as I can remember, evangelical Christians have insisted that the Bible be interpreted according to its plain meaning. Other parts of Christianity have suggested that the creation story in Genesis, in which God creates the entire universe, including humans, in six days and then rests on the seventh, can be interpreted symbolically, thus avoiding direct conflict with modern science. But evangelicals have held firm. If the Bible says six days, it means six days! Likewise, if the Bible says Jesus walked on water, he literally walked on water. If the Bible says that a virgin girl named Mary conceived Jesus because the Spirit of God impregnated her, then that's precisely what happened. You see my point...

In the last few years, however, some evangelical Christian writers have wanted to change this approach to interpreting the Bible to the point where they have completely undermined the direct teachings and example of Jesus! Here I am referring to writers who have attacked empathy and Christian love, claiming that empathy is toxic. One example they suggest is that too much empathy for someone yearning to become transgender might make us feel so much sympathy that we end up supporting sinful behavior. So, according to them, empathy and love must always be balanced against God's call for righteousness. If love and righteousness oppose one another, then righteousness must always win.

Yet in the large majority of cases in the Bible, God's call for righteousness *is* a call for love! If righteousness always wins, the Prodigal Son comes home to a closed door. If righteousness always wins, then Jesus doesn't teach forgiving not just seven times, but seventy times seven. Instead, he teaches no forgiveness at all. If righteousness always wins, Jesus doesn't go to the cross for sinners because it's God's will that they be damned!

As I look at our current situation, those who preach toxic empathy do so because they know perfectly well it's the only way to excuse Donald Trump and his contribution to the cause of Christian nationalism. As we will see very shortly in a book summary, and then again in a long exploration of Donald Trump's behavior as president in Chapter Six, those who want to take away the plain truth of Jesus' teachings and the example of his life are doing so to take power over our nation and use that power to become very rich. They have their reasons, and they may be able to fool many of their followers. I do not believe they will fool God, however. When Jesus taught that it is easier for a camel to go through the eye of a needle than for a rich person to enter the Kingdom of God, he put his finger on the tremendous temptation of wealth in this life. And when he asked what profit it could ever be for us to gain the whole world if we lose our souls in the bargain, he showed us the eternal stakes involved. As I will say several times in the chapters ahead, God will not be mocked or fooled.

If you think toxic empathy is a good excuse to not take Jesus at his word, then this may not be the book for you. If we can go forward taking the Bible in the plain way that Jesus shows us in his life and teachings, then let us let the Bible be the answer to all our questions.

With that agreement, let's begin by carefully looking at what the Bible says about judgment and hell. Our aim is to remember the most important teachings of the Bible. Our purpose is to reflect on our best understanding of God's expectations for how we are supposed to live. And at the end, we will seek to discover how we can experience eternal life in this present life, as Jesus promises in the Gospel of John.

In the end, my hope is that our reflections will help us *fall in love with Jesus* and understand how we can help continue his ministry and help birth the kingdom of God in all its fullness. Let's begin with a summary of the whole book so you can see if you want to dive in.

Maybe I have your attention, but before you read a lot of pages you would rather cut to the chase and see the main points we are going to consider. Then if you are still interested you can dive in for a closer look. If you already want to dive in, you can skip this summary and go straight to Chapter One.

We have already agreed on the first point. Our final authority is the Bible. We agree that the Bible is the inerrant word of God and that it provides all the wisdom we need to live the life that God intends for us. If we are uncertain about something, the Bible will be the voice of God.

Point two. The Bible holds that God is the ultimate authority in the universe and in our lives. God created the universe through Jesus, the creative Word (logos) that God spoke to call the different parts of the universe and our world into being. As the Apostle Paul said, "In God we live and move and have our being." (Acts 17:28 New International Version) So, we live within God's larger life and are sustained by God's Spirit. Since we owe our existence to God, no human being or human government can replace God's authority. We take our marching orders from God. God does not take marching orders from us.

Point three. The Bible teaches us that God has ordained that Jesus will judge us at some point after we die. There is no hiding how we have lived from Jesus. God and Jesus know whether our faith is sincere or is only lip service. There is no fooling God and Jesus, because they know us better than we know ourselves.

Point four. The Bible teaches that Christ's judgment will deliver us either to eternal life with God in heaven, or to eternal death. In Matthew, Mark, and Luke, Jesus tells us that those who do not go to heaven go to hell – a place of fire and torment. John does not record Jesus as describing a place of eternal torment, but records Jesus saying that we will receive eternal life and light or eternal death and darkness.

Point five. The Bible teaches that Christ will judge us based on whether we have done God's will by loving God, loving others – especially those who are struggling -- and loving ourselves. This can be seen in the way that God reaches out to God's people, both in the Old Testament and in the New Testament. In the Old Testament, the most important story is God calling and helping Moses to lead God's people out of slavery in Egypt and then eventually leading them to inhabit a new Promised Land. In that land, God intends them to establish a faithful, just, and loving nation that is a blessing to all the people of the earth. In the New Testament, the most important story is God working through the birth, life, ministry, death, and resurrection of Jesus to lead God's people out of the state of sin – which in the Bible means separation from God in which fear and selfishness come to dominate our lives – and into the state of eternal life where we are free from the power of sin and death in the new Promised Land of Heaven. In both cases God reaches out in love to bring people who are struggling into a place where they can thrive.

Point six. The Bible provides very specific instructions on who God intends us to include as we help to bring God's love into the world. As we just saw, the overall theme of the Bible is God working to save God's people. In the Old Testament, God leads God's people out of slavery in Egypt into a promised land on this earth. In the New Testament God leads God's people out of slavery to sin and death into a new promised land in heaven. In the whole of the Bible, God is especially concerned for those in greatest need. Those who live under oppression or who are being taken advantage of by their employers. Those who are foreigners in the land. Those who are hungry, thirsty, in need of clothes, sick or in prison. Those who are children. Both the prophets and Jesus himself are crystal clear that God's people must help everyone in these kinds of need. In the entire Bible, verse after verse insists upon this.

Point seven. The Bible teaches that no human person – except Jesus – is or was perfect. Moreover, God loves us and Christ's Spirit is constantly at work in our lives to help us grow in love. Therefore, God and Jesus are not eager to send us to hell or allow us to die in darkness. Yet we are the ones who are supposed to be working for God, and Jesus' ultimate judgment of our lives keeps us honest. Many Christians focus on the redemptive power of Jesus' death to save us from the power of sin and evil. Theologically, they see Jesus going to the cross as taking upon himself the punishment that should have come to them, so that God can release them from wrongdoing and bring them with Jesus into heaven. Their belief in this comes from John 3:16-17 where Jesus famously says, "For this is how God loved the world: He gave his one and only Son, so that everyone who believes in him will not perish but have eternal life. God sent his Son into the world not to judge the world, but to save the world through him." New Living Translation (Remember this is the main version of the Bible we are using – going forward, if no version is cited the version will be the NLT.)

Perhaps this passage seems like a "get out of jail card." We may be tempted to think, "If I just believe in Jesus then all my sins are forgiven, so that anything I do or don't do will be overlooked by Jesus on the day of my judgment." Yet there are many levels of belief. I can believe that Saturn has rings, but it makes no real difference in my life. That level of "belief" is not going to save me if my bad deeds reveal a much stronger belief that I am entitled to take advantage of others and ignore Jesus' direct teachings.

God and Jesus will not be mocked or fooled. Casual belief in Jesus is not some parlor trick to get us into heaven. True belief in Jesus means falling in love with him, allowing him to guide our lives, and living out the sacrificial love that he lived. Here are his words in Matthew 16:24b-27: "If any of you wants to be my follower, you must give up your own way, take up your cross, and follow me. If you try to hang on to your life, you will lose it. But if you give up your life for my sake, you will save it. And what do you benefit if you gain the whole world but lose your own soul? Is anything worth more than your soul? For the Son of Man will come with his angels in the glory of his Father and will judge all people according to their deeds." Jesus loved and helped known sinners. He touched and healed people who were considered unclean. See the Parable of the Sheep and the Goats in Matthew 25:31-46 for a detailed description of the behavior Jesus expects and the judgment that waits for those who do – and those who do not – meet his expectations. John 3:16 is not a "get out of jail card."

Point eight. Donald Trump's deeds cannot be supported by anyone who truly believes in Jesus and is trying to carry on his works of love. There is a stark, unmistakable contrast between Jesus' ministry of love for those on the margins and Donald Trump's aggressive attempts to take as much power and wealth for himself as he possibly can while continually working to make the upper 1% in the United States wealthier at the expense of the poorest people in the U. S. and the world. To gain favor with evangelicals, Donald Trump, has sided with them on positions like severely limiting abortions or keeping transgender people from serving in the military or competing in sports. However, because a leader does some things that we personally favor – or even that we believe are ordained by God -- we will not please God by ignoring the vast number of things that flout God's expectations.

So, what is Trump doing that is bad in the eyes of God? A much fuller explanation will be given in Chapter Six, but here let's look quickly at two examples:

First, Trump's policies are harming and killing a huge number of children. One of the first things he did upon taking office in 2025 was to work with Elon Musk to defund and destroy the United States Agency for International Development (USAID). Since this is the main way we offer nonmilitary assistance to poor countries, it immediately ended crucial food aid to children starving in Sudan and other nations with no plan in place to help them through other programs. Within a few days children started dying. The abrupt end of funds put at least 14 million children at risk of losing nutritional support and lifesaving interventions in 2025. It also ended maternal and child health programs, reduced access to clean water and sanitation in schools, disrupted protection services for children vulnerable to sex trafficking and forced labor, and threatened access to healthcare for 95 million people worldwide including access to vaccines and treatment for malaria. It affected 177 countries. A November 2025 article in the New Yorker Daily estimated that *600,000 people had already died because of the loss of US-AID, two-thirds of them children.* Projections by the UCLA Fielding School of Public Health released on July 2, 2025, estimate that if U.S. AID is not refunded there will be more than 14 million deaths globally by 2030. This includes 4.5 million children under the age of five, or about 700,000 child deaths annually. Jesus taught us that children are the greatest in the kingdom of God and that it would be better for anyone harming them to have a millstone tied around their neck and be thrown into the depths of the sea than to face God's judgment. (See Matthew 18:6) Can you imagine any Christian standing next to Donald Trump or Elon Musk on the days they face Christ's judgment and holding up a hand saying, "Yes. I supported them ending USAID. I didn't care about the children who died."

Second, Trump's advocacy for and ultimate passage of the so-called "One Big Beautiful Bill Act" has the federal government taking money from the poor and giving it to the richest 1% of the population at a time when the income division between the rich and poor is already the highest in U.S. history. Specifically, it causes cuts of $491 billion dollars from Medicare between the years 2027 to 2034. It also cuts nearly 1 trillion dollars from Medicaid over the next ten years, causing 310,000 people to lose their health insurance. Because rural hospitals depend on Medicaid to fund treatment for so many of their patients, many rural hospitals across the nation have been closing, leaving all their residents far away from a hospital. The same is true of nursing homes. Another result of the bill is that families in the bottom 10% of the population will lose about $1,600 annually worth of food aid and Medicaid in the years between 2026 and 2034. It will also cut funding for schools and childcare programs. Meanwhile the benefit to those in the bottom 20% of the population will be an average tax cut of $90 per year. Those in the top 1% will see their taxes lowered by between $64,000 and $90,000 a year. Jesus taught us that we cannot serve both God and money at the same time. (See Matthew 6:24 in the Sermon on the Mount) If you read Jesus' Parable of the Rich Man and Lazarus, you will see how it turns out for those who are rich and refuse to help the poor who live literally on their doorstep. (See Luke 16:19-31) If you believe in the Bible and support Donald Trump and his policies of favoring the rich and taking from the poor, you are begging Jesus to send you to hell.

These examples are two of the most obvious, but to get a sense of how overwhelmingly Donald Trump's policies run completely against God's teachings in the Bible, please read Chapter Six.

This is the bare bones warning contained in this book. Again, I take no pleasure in writing it and I want you and all people to thrive. I hope you will dive in and read everything, because there is much more to say. In the Gospel of John, eternal life is both a present and a future experience. In Chapter Seven we will explore what eternal life in this present moment feels like, and how you can know that you are on the right track. Conversely, in Chapter Eight we will explore how it may feel if you are on the track to be sent to hell. And finally, in the last chapter we will return to falling in love with Jesus, feeling his constant guiding presence, and letting him lead us from death to eternal life.

1

Jesus, Judgment, and Hell

Did you know that the word in the New Testament that Jesus uses most to describe hell comes from an actual place? Jesus' word is "Gehenna". Gehenna comes from the Hebrew phrase גֵּיא בֶן־הִנֹּם. This sounds in English like "gē ben-hinnōm", and it directly translates to "valley of the son of Hinnom". This was a real valley located southwest of Jerusalem, which was used as both a garbage dump and a place of ritual human sacrifices to the god Moloch, making it a symbol of impurity and judgment. Both garbage and human bodies were burned there, so it was a flaming, stinking place. Over time, Gehenna came to be used synonymously with "hell" or "inferno," meaning a place of fiery punishment. When Jesus begins his preaching ministry, he uses Gehenna to picture the eternal punishment awaiting those who reject God's will.

Let's have a look at places in the Bible where Jesus talks about judgment and hell, beginning in the Gospels of Matthew, Mark, and Luke, whose authors drew from common sources. In the next chapter, we will look at how Jesus pictures judgment and hell in the Gospel of John, which was written from a different perspective with some different sources.

In the Sermon on the Mount

In Matthew, the first time Jesus talks about going to hell is in his famous Sermon on the Mount. In Matthew 5:21-22, Jesus says: "You have heard that our ancestors were told, 'You must not murder. If you commit murder, you are subject to judgment.' But I say, if you are even angry with someone, you are subject to judgment! If you call someone an idiot, you are in danger of being brought before the court. And if you curse someone, you are in danger of the fires of hell."

Here, Jesus begins by referring to the sixth law of the Ten Commandments, "You must not murder" (Exodus 20:13 and Deuteronomy 5:17). This commandment carries God's judgment against anyone who commits murder. Jesus, however, teaches us to go even further and practice deep kindness in our everyday lives. He warns us about the consequences of anger and tells us that if we curse someone, we put ourselves in danger of being sent to the fires of hell (Gehenna).

Still in the Sermon on the Mount, we come to Matthew 5:27-30 where Jesus refers to the seventh commandment and says: "You have heard the commandment that says, 'You must not commit adultery.' But I say, anyone who even looks at a woman with lust has already committed adultery with her in his heart. So if your eye—even your good eye—causes you to lust, gouge it out and throw it away. It is better for you to lose one part of your body than for your whole body to be thrown into hell. And if your hand—even your stronger hand—causes you to sin, cut it off and throw it away. It is better for you to lose one part of your body than for your whole body to be thrown into hell."

Wow! Very few of us have followed this teaching literally! But this is another strong sign that Jesus is very serious about his followers living in a quite different spiritual reality than the Judeo-Christian tradition ever expressed before. Jesus does not want men to see women as bodies to be used for their personal pleasure, but as children of God created to fulfill God's purpose. Therefore, they are loved by God and of infinite worth. They are entitled to live their lives free from men molesting them, physically or verbally. So Jesus teaches us directly that if we use others as mere objects to please ourselves, we risk being thrown into the fires of hell (Gehenna).

Sending his disciples to do the ministry of God's reign

The next time Jesus talks about judgment and hell in Matthew is when he sends his disciples out to minister to the villages of Israel. The Gospel of Matthew was written about 80 years after Jesus' death and resurrection. It was during a time of conflict between those in the Jewish community who were coming to believe that Jesus was God's Messiah and others who rejected the idea that God's Messiah could end up crucified and die a criminal's death. This story, which forms the tenth chapter of Matthew, dramatically reflects that conflict. Jesus tells his disciples to go on their mission with no provisions at all – no money, not even a walking stick or a change of clothes. He says, "Go and announce that the Kingdom of Heaven is near. Heal the sick, raise the dead, cure those with leprosy, and cast out demons. Give as freely as you have received!" (Matthew 10:7-8)

But Jesus also warns them that they will encounter rejection. He says, "Look, I am sending you out as sheep among wolves. So be as shrewd as snakes and harmless as doves. But beware! For you will be handed over to the courts and will be flogged with whips in the synagogues. You will stand trial before governors and kings because you are my followers. But this will be your opportunity to tell the rulers and other unbelievers about me. When you are arrested, don't worry about how to respond or what to say. God will give you the right words at the right time. For it is not you who will be speaking—it will be the Spirit of your Father speaking through you." (Matthew 10:16-20)

Through it all, Jesus tells his disciples to be brave. "Don't be afraid of those who want to kill your body; they cannot touch your soul. Fear only God, who can destroy both soul and body in hell. (Matthew 10:28)

This is nothing less than Jesus' teaching about the most important principle for life. As Jesus' disciples, we cannot fear human beings (or any other earthly thing). Our lives are eternal, and no matter what danger we face, the truth of God's love revealed in the birth, life, ministry, death, and resurrection of Jesus is our polar star. In all experiences, we must stay faithful to God. As Jesus says just a few verses later, "If you refuse to take up your cross and follow me, you are not worthy of being mine. If you cling to your life, you will lose it; but if you give up your life for me, you will find it." (Matthew 10:38-39) Jesus is teaching us that, like his disciples, we have a mission to embody the reign of God which is breaking into human life and we must allow nothing – not even our human fears of getting hurt – to stop us from expressing it. Jesus believes that we will have a time of reckoning with God and that we must face God's divine judgment.

In the Parable of the Wheat and the Weeds

Continuing further in Matthew with Jesus' teachings about judgment and going to hell, the next passage comes in chapter 13. In this chapter, Matthew includes many of Jesus' parables, which are stories that make a sharp spiritual point. In verses 24 through 30, Jesus tells the Parable of the Wheat and the Weeds. As Jesus pictures it, a farmer prepares a field and plants it with good wheat seed. But that night, an enemy comes and overplants it with weeds. As the seeds begin to grow, a sharp-eyed servant spots the difference between the kinds of plants that are sprouting. He goes to the farmer and asks how this could have happened. "An enemy has done this!" the farmer exclaims. "What should we do," asks the servant, "pull the weeds up now?" "No," the farmer decides. "The good plants will get pulled up with the bad. Let them grow up together and we'll separate them at the harvest. Then we'll tie the weeds in bundles and burn them. The wheat we will store in the barn."

Later, in verses 36 to 43, Jesus explains the parable to his disciples. "The Son of Man (Jesus' name for himself as their leader) is the farmer who plants the good seed. The field is the world, and the good seed represents the people of the Kingdom. The weeds are the people who belong to the evil one. The enemy who planted the weeds among the wheat is the devil. The harvest is the end of the world, and the harvesters are the angels. Just as the weeds are sorted out and burned in the fire, so it will be at the end of the world. The Son of Man will send his angels, and they will remove from his Kingdom everything that causes sin and all who do evil. And the angels will throw them into the fiery furnace, where there will be weeping and gnashing of teeth. Then the righteous will shine like the sun in their Father's Kingdom. Anyone with ears to hear should listen and understand!"

Once again, Jesus pictures a world with both good and bad people living together. At the end of the world, a day of judgment will come, and under the direction of the Son of Man (Jesus), the angels will separate the good and the bad. The bad will be thrown into the fiery furnace of Gehenna. As Jesus cautions, anyone with ears to hear the meaning of his teachings – especially those of us who claim to be his followers -- should listen and understand.

When the disciples wonder who is the greatest in God's kingdom

The next passage in Matthew, where Jesus talks about hell, has to do with children. Matthew, Mark, and Luke all record the disciples wondering about who will be considered greatest in the kingdom of heaven. In Matthew, they ask Jesus directly, and in Mark and Luke, they argue among themselves until Jesus sets them straight. In each instance, Jesus uses a child to teach them. Here is the story in Matthew 18:1-10:

At that time, the disciples came to Jesus and asked, "Who, then, is the greatest in the kingdom of heaven?" He called a little child to him and placed the child among them. And he said: "Truly I tell you, unless you change and become like little children, you will never enter the kingdom of heaven. Therefore, whoever takes the lowly position of this child is the greatest in the kingdom of heaven. And whoever welcomes one such child in my name welcomes me.

"If anyone causes one of these little ones—those who believe in me—to stumble, it would be better for them to have a large millstone hung around their neck and to be drowned in the depths of the sea. Woe to the world because of the things that cause people to stumble! Such things must come, but woe to the person through whom they come! If your hand or foot causes you to stumble, cut it off and throw it away. It is better for you to enter life maimed or crippled than to have two hands or two feet and be thrown into eternal fire (Gehenna). And if your eye causes you to stumble, gouge it out and throw it away. It is better for you to enter life with one eye than to have two eyes and be thrown into the fire of hell (Gehenna).

"See that you do not despise one of these little ones. For I tell you that their angels in heaven always see the face of my Father in heaven."

In Jesus' time, the common expectation was that the greatest person was an old man who was wealthy and powerful. The High Priest in Jerusalem, or a wealthy landowner out in the villages, would be the ones most people would call great. Young children would be at the very bottom of the list.

As is often the case, Jesus stands the expectations of the world upside-down. Those who think a lot of themselves can't even enter the kingdom of heaven because they can't see their need for God. According to Jesus, to enter the kingdom, we must take the lowly position of a child and not think so highly of ourselves. And we must welcome children, for when we do, we welcome Christ.

If we cause a child to stumble... woe be unto us! Jesus declares it will be like having a millstone tied to our neck and then being thrown into the depths of the sea. And – here it is again -- if our hands, feet, or eyes cause us to stumble, we would do better to cut them off and enter the kingdom maimed than to be thrown into the eternal fire.

Mark's portrayal of hell

When Mark tells this same account of Jesus teaching his disciples about who is greatest in the kingdom of heaven by using a child, Jesus puts even more emphasis on the terrible nature of hell by saying first that "the fires of hell never go out", and second by quoting part of Isaiah 66:24 where Isaiah says that, "the worms that eat [God's enemies] do not die and the fire that burns them is not quenched." (See Mark 9:36-37 and 42-48)

In the Woes Against the Pharisees

Back to Matthew. In Chapter 23, Jesus goes on a rampage against religious leaders known as the Pharisees. Their name, "Pharisees," means those who are set apart. In Jesus' time, they were set apart by taking special pride in following the letter of Jewish law, including dietary restrictions, observance of the Sabbath day of rest, and maintaining ritual purity by not touching anything unclean. The Pharisees were certain that Jesus could not be sent by God because he ate with sinners, allowed his disciples to pluck grain on the Sabbath, and touched and healed people who were ritually unclean, such as a leper or a woman with a flow of menstrual blood. For his part, Jesus saw them as hypocrites who tried to look better than everyone else but failed to practice the kindness and love toward those in need that God expects. In a series of sayings in Chapter 23, Jesus lets them have it! Among other things, he calls them "Blind Guides", "Hypocrites", "White-Washed Tombs", and "Snakes and Broods of Vipers". We can see why they joined other religious leaders in wanting Jesus put to death!

To say a little more about what Jesus didn't like, he saw the Pharisees emphasizing outward conformity and neglecting the weightier matters of the law, such as justice, mercy, and faithfulness. He said, "Blind guides! You strain your water so you won't accidentally swallow a gnat, but you swallow a camel!" (Matthew 23:24). He accused them of parading around looking very fine like painted-up tombstones, but inside they were full of decaying bones and everything unclean. He claimed they would kill real prophets and teachers just as their ancestors did. In fact, Jesus asks them directly, "How will you escape being condemned to hell?" (Matthew 23:33)

In the Parable of the Sheep and the Goats

The last place in Matthew where Jesus refers directly to judgment and hell is in one of his most famous parables, the Parable of the Sheep and the Goats, which we find in Matthew 25:31-46. As a refresher, let's read it from the beginning:

"When the Son of Man comes in his glory, and all the angels with him, he will sit on his glorious throne. All the nations will be gathered before him, and he will separate the people one from another as a shepherd separates the sheep from the goats. He will put the sheep on his right and the goats on his left.

"Then the King will say to those on his right, 'Come, you who are blessed by my Father; take your inheritance, the kingdom prepared for you since the creation of the world. For I was hungry and you gave me something to eat, I was thirsty and you gave me something to drink, I was a stranger and you invited me in, I needed clothes and you clothed me, I was sick and you looked after me, I was in prison and you came to visit me.'

"Then the righteous will answer him, 'Lord, when did we see you hungry and feed you, or thirsty and give you something to drink? When did we see you a stranger and invite you in, or needing clothes and clothe you? When did we see you sick or in prison and go to visit you?'

"The King will reply, 'Truly I tell you, whatever you did for one of the least of these brothers and sisters of mine, you did for me.'

"Then he will say to those on his left, 'Depart from me, you who are cursed, into the eternal fire prepared for the devil and his angels. For I was hungry and you gave me nothing to eat, I was thirsty and you gave me nothing to drink, I was a stranger and you did not invite me in, I needed clothes and you did not clothe me, I was sick and in prison and you did not look after me.'

"They also will answer, 'Lord, when did we see you hungry or thirsty or a stranger or needing clothes or sick or in prison, and did not help you?'

"He will reply, 'Truly I tell you, whatever you did not do for one of the least of these, you did not do for me.'

"Then they will go away to eternal punishment, but the righteous to eternal life."

Here in this last passage of Matthew, we see three things that are becoming increasingly familiar.

First, we will all face a time of judgment. Jesus will know what we have done with our lives, and we will receive what is appropriate.

Second, if we are sent to hell, it will be a place of eternal fire and punishment with no escape.

And third, appearances will not make up for actions. Putting on a show, like the Pharisees, will not impress God. Being seen by other humans as powerful, important, or religious will not impress God. Being truly kind, truly merciful and helpful, and truly just will matter. It is fascinating that neither the sheep or the goats recognize that they have either given or failed to give help to the King. Neither group can remember encountering him when he needed help. Yet he tells them both: whatever you did or didn't do with the least of these my brothers and sisters, you did it – or you didn't do it – to me.

Judgment and Hell in the Gospel of Luke

The Gospel of Luke was written slightly later than Matthew and is mainly addressed to non-Jewish, Greek-speaking people who are coming to believe that Jesus is God's Messiah and joining Christian churches. So Luke does not use the word "Gehenna" with its Jewish roots. Instead, he uses the word "Hades" which is Greek in origin and means the underworld where the souls of the dead reside. Like Matthew, Luke also records Jesus using parables and stories to teach his listeners spiritual truths. Matthew includes parables like "The Sheep and the Goats," which Luke does not have. And Luke includes others, like the Parable of the Prodigal Son, or the Parable of the Good Samaritan, which Matthew does not have. Another story that Luke recounts Jesus telling is the story of the Rich Man and Lazarus in Luke 16:19-31.

Its picture of heaven and hell is quite striking. Let's have a close look. Jesus says:

"There was a rich man who was dressed in purple and fine linen and lived in luxury every day. At his gate was laid a beggar named Lazarus, covered with sores and longing to eat what fell from the rich man's table. Even the dogs came and licked his sores.

"The time came when the beggar died and the angels carried him to Abraham's side. The rich man also died and was buried. In Hades, where he was in torment, he looked up and saw Abraham far away, with Lazarus by his side. So he called to him, 'Father Abraham, have pity on me and send Lazarus to dip the tip of his finger in water and cool my tongue, because I am in agony in this fire.'

"But Abraham replied, 'Son, remember that in your lifetime you received your good things, while Lazarus received bad things, but now he is comforted here and you are in agony. And besides all this, between us and you a great chasm has been set in place, so that those who want to go from here to you cannot, nor can anyone cross over from there to us.'

"He answered, 'Then I beg you, father, send Lazarus to my family, for I have five brothers. Let him warn them, so that they will not also come to this place of torment.'

"Abraham replied, 'They have Moses and the Prophets; let them listen to them.'

"'No, father Abraham,' he said, 'but if someone from the dead goes to them, they will repent.'

"He said to him, 'If they do not listen to Moses and the Prophets, they will not be convinced even if someone rises from the dead.'"

Oh my. The irony in these words hits hard! Let us hope and pray that we are not as blind as the rich man and his brothers.

Summary

These are the only times in the Gospels of Matthew, Mark, and Luke where Jesus teaches us directly about divine judgment and the nature of hell. In every instance, what Jesus says will lead him to condemn people to hell is behavior that is not kind or loving to people on the margins who need our love the most.

Reflection Questions

1. How and when in your life did you first hear about hell?

2. What sense did it make to you back then?

3. As you reflect on Jesus' teachings about judgment and hell in this chapter, how do they make you feel?

4. Do you feel certain that you will not end up in hell, or does going to hell feel like a possibility that you need to take seriously?

5. What are the main standards you believe Jesus will use to judge your life?

2

Judgment and John's Gospel

The Gospel of John is the latest gospel to be written and is very different from the others. Mark is written about 70CE, then Matthew about 10 years later, and Luke a little later than that. John is the last gospel to be written, about 120CE. As we will see, John has a distinct voice, and a highly developed theological understanding of Jesus' relationship to God. In John, Jesus clearly pictures God's expectations for us as his followers and shows us the consequences of what happens when we do meet those expectations... and what happens when we don't. Jesus gives no descriptions of hell in John like those in the other gospels. But God's judgment and potential wrath are certainly there.

John's picture of Jesus as the Son of God
Mark, the earliest and shortest gospel, begins with the story of John the Baptist and goes on from there. When he is baptized by John, Jesus comes up out of the water of the Jordan River, sees the heavens torn open and the Holy Spirit descending upon him like a dove, and then hears God's voice saying to him, "You are my dearly loved Son, and you bring me great joy." (Mark 1:10-11)

Matthew tells a big part of the Christmas story, including the angel Gabriel's visit to Mary, Joseph's dreams, the visit of the magi, and the need for Joseph to take his family into Egypt to escape the mass murder of baby boys by Herod's troops after the magi reveal to him that a new king has been born.

Luke tells another big part of the Christmas story, including Gabriel's visit to Mary, Mary going to see her kinswoman Elizabeth who is pregnant with John the Baptist, Jesus' birth in Bethlehem and the angels' announcement of his birth to shepherds, who immediately leave their flocks and come to worship Jesus.

John adds another dimension entirely. John begins not in Israel at the time when Jesus is born. Instead, John begins all the way back to when God creates the universe as it is told in the first two chapters of the Book of Genesis. Let's read John's profound words in John 1:1-18:

"In the beginning the Word already existed.
   The Word was with God,
   and the Word was God.
   He existed in the beginning with God.
   God created everything through him,
     and nothing was created except through him.
   The Word gave life to everything,
     and nothing that was created was created except through him
     and his life brought light to everyone.
   The light shines in the darkness,
     and the darkness can never extinguish it.

"God sent a man, John the Baptist, to tell about the light so that everyone might believe because of his testimony. John himself was not the light; he was simply a witness to tell about the light. The one who is the true light, who gives light to everyone, was coming into the world.

"He came into the very world he created, but the world didn't recognize him. He came to his own people, and even they rejected him. But to all who believed him and accepted him, he gave the right to become children of God. They are reborn—not with a physical birth resulting from human passion or plan, but a birth that comes from God.

"So the Word became human and made his home among us. He was full of unfailing love and faithfulness [grace and truth in other translations]. And we have seen his glory, the glory of the Father's one and only Son.

"John testified about him when he shouted to the crowds, "This is the one I was talking about when I said, 'Someone is coming after me who is far greater than I am, for he existed long before me.'"

"From his abundance we have all received one gracious blessing after another. For the law was given through Moses, but God's unfailing love and faithfulness [grace and truth] came through Jesus Christ. No one has ever seen God. But the unique One, who is himself God, is near to the Father's heart. He has revealed God to us."

These first 18 verses are called the Prologue to the Gospel of John because they present us with several theological ideas that John will return to repeatedly. These are:

Jesus is truly and fully God and was present with God from the beginning of time. Jesus knows about God's eternal realm and is the only one who can accurately testify about its nature.

Jesus is the Word that the first creation story in the Book of Genesis describes God speaking when God creates the universe out of primeval chaos. The Greek word that John uses when he says that Jesus is the Word is "logos" which means the power of things to stick together and be something, rather than chaotic.

Jesus is the Word that God uses to call the universe into order and all of it, every individual thing, is created by Jesus. John also says that in Jesus is life and that his life brings light to all people. John says Jesus' light is indestructible. The light shines in the darkness and the darkness cannot extinguish it.

Yet Jesus encounters a problem with recognition. God sends John the Baptist to announce the coming of the light. Then the Word becomes flesh in the person of Jesus and God sends Jesus, the light bearer, into the world. Yet many fail to recognize Jesus. Even his own people (the Jewish people) fail to recognize him. Although he has created them, they don't see and recognize that Jesus is God's Son and the Messiah they have been waiting for.

Yet some do see his glorious light, recognize him and become reborn, receiving grace upon grace – or as the NLT puts it, they receive God's unfailing love and faithfulness.

In the end, John shows that God has sent Jesus to us so that we humans can come into a life-giving relationship with God. And the way that we do that is to recognize that everything we need to know about God is revealed to us by Jesus. As John puts it at the end of his Prologue: "The law was given through Moses, but God's unfailing love and faithfulness [grace and truth] came through Jesus Christ. No one has ever seen God. But the unique One, who is himself God, is near to the Father's heart. He has revealed God to us."

Once we recognize who Jesus is and truly believe in him, we are spiritually reborn. We "become children of God. [We] are reborn—not with a physical birth resulting from human passion or plan, but a birth that comes from God."

Everything Turns on Recognizing Jesus

In John, everything turns on whether we recognize that Jesus is God's Son and that he is the key to living in God's eternal kingdom (or domain). Human beings – and all other creatures and things that have been created -- have been created through Jesus' power to stick things together. Therefore, all humans carry Jesus' light. Yet there is this problem of recognition.

When John's gospel was written, the conflict between Jews who accepted Jesus as God's Messiah and Jews who rejected him was ongoing. So, over and over in John's account, people want to know who Jesus really is and what his true relationship with God is. (We will look carefully at the story of Nicodemus, but others include the woman at the well, a man born blind who Jesus heals, Mary and Martha, the Pharisees and Chief Priests who decide Jesus must die, Pontius Pilate, Jesus' disciple Philip just before Jesus' death, even "Doubting Thomas", who struggles after Jesus' resurrection.)

For John, Jesus is the key to entering an authentic relationship with God. The way John puts it in the Prologue and elsewhere in the gospel is that by recognizing and believing that Jesus is God's Son, we can be born anew – reborn spiritually, not physically -- and reborn so that we live united with God's love and light. When we are reborn in this way we begin to experience eternal life (or life in God's domain) even before we die. So eternal life is a present, as well as a future, reality. When we believe in Jesus, God's Spirit enters us and becomes the motivating power of our lives. We become followers of Jesus who carry on his ministry. In John 14:12-14 Jesus tells his followers that after he dies and returns to heaven to be with God, they will do even greater things than he did! This empowers his ministry to continue, and ensures that new people will be spiritually reborn to carry out his command to "love one another as I have loved you." (John 15:12)

An Experience of Recognizing Jesus

Frederica Matthewes-Green, a well-known author and speaker in the Greek Orthodox Church, recalls her first encounter with Jesus at a time when she was a recently married young adult traveling with her husband Gary in Ireland. She had drifted out of her childhood Christianity and was practicing Hinduism when she and Gary visited an old church. Here is her story:

"In a block of business buildings we came upon a church and decided to go inside for a look; even declared Hindus can't travel Europe without being exposed to some church architecture. I strolled around the dimly lit building, admiring stained glass windows and stonework. Eventually I came upon a small side altar. Above it there was a white marble statue of Jesus with his arms held low and open, and his heart exposed on his chest, twined with thorns and springing with flames. This depicts an apparition to a French nun in 1675; she heard Jesus say, 'Behold the heart which has so loved mankind.'

"I can't really explain what happened next. I was standing there looking at the statue, and then I discovered I was on my knees. I could hear an interior voice speaking to me. Not with my ears -- it was more like a radio inside suddenly clicked on. The voice was both intimate and authoritative, and it filled me.

"It said, 'I am your life. You think that your life is your name, your personality, your history. But that is not your life. I am your life.' It went on, naming that "life force" notion I admired: 'Beyond that, you think that your life is the fact that you are alive, that your breath goes in and out, that energy courses in your veins. But even that is not your life. I am your life.'

'I am the foundation of everything else in your life.'

"I stood up feeling pretty shaky. It was like sitting quietly in your living room and having the roof blown off. I didn't have any doubt who the "I" was that was speaking to me, and it wasn't someone I was eager to get to know. If someone had asked me a half-hour earlier, I would have said I was not sure the fellow had ever lived. Yet here he was, and though I didn't know him it seemed he already knew me, from the deepest inside out. I kept quiet about this for a week, trying to figure it out. I didn't even tell Gary, though he must have wondered why my eyebrows kept hovering up near my hairline.

"This wasn't one of those woo-woo spiritual experiences where everything goes misty and the next day you wonder if it really happened. It was shockingly real, as if I'd encountered a dimension of reality I'd never known existed before. Years later I read C. S. Lewis' novella, *The Great Divorce*, which begins with the charming idea that every day a bus crosses the great divide from hell to heaven. Anyone who wants can go, and anyone who wants can stay. The thing is, heaven hurts. It's too real. The visitors from hell can't walk on the grass, because the blades pierce their feet like knives. It takes time to grow real enough to endure heaven, a process of unflinching self-discovery and repentance that few are willing to take. At the end of the day, most of the tourists get back on the bus to hell.

"This experience in the church was real like that, like grass that pierces your feet. In that explosive moment I found that Jesus was realer than anything I'd ever encountered, the touchstone of reality. It left me with a great hunger for more, so that my whole life is leaning toward him, questing for him, striving to break down the walls inside that shelter me from his gaze. I am looking for him all my life."

Becoming Born Again From Above

As I listen to people talk about their spiritual growth and as I reflect on my own walk with Jesus, I must say that Frederica Matthewes-Green's experience is more sudden and direct than most people experience, but it shows us how Jesus – who according to the Gospel of John creates each one of us – is the true center and foundation of our lives. Whether we are consciously aware of Jesus or not, he and his purpose for living are deep within all of us because it is his power as the divine logos that creates us. As John says, Jesus' life is the light of our lives, and we must choose whether to live in his light or to seek to hide in darkness.

As we noted before, John tells many stories in his gospel of people who are wondering who Jesus is and are trying to recognize him. An early and dramatic story that John tells is the story of Nicodemus, a Pharisee who comes to visit Jesus in the cover of night (darkness).

Like John's Prologue, it will help us to read it from John 3:1-21:

"There was a man named Nicodemus, a Jewish religious leader who was a Pharisee. After dark one evening, he came to speak with Jesus. 'Rabbi,' he said, 'we all know that God has sent you to teach us. Your miraculous signs are evidence that God is with you.'"

Jesus replied, "I tell you the truth, unless you are born again, you cannot see the Kingdom of God." [Another translation puts this sentence: "As God is my witness, no one can enter God's domain without being born again from above." The Scholars Version (SV)]

"What do you mean?" exclaimed Nicodemus. "How can an old man go back into his mother's womb and be born again?"

Jesus replied, "I assure you, no one can enter the Kingdom of God without being born of water and the Spirit. Humans can reproduce only human life, but the Holy Spirit gives birth to spiritual life. So don't be surprised when I say, 'You must be born again.' The wind blows wherever it wants. Just as you can hear the wind but can't tell where it comes from or where it is going, so you can't explain how people are born of the Spirit."

"How are these things possible?" Nicodemus asked.

Jesus replied, "You are a respected Jewish teacher, and yet you don't understand these things? I assure you, we tell you what we know and have seen, and yet you won't believe our testimony. But if you don't believe me when I tell you about earthly things, how can you possibly believe if I tell you about heavenly things? No one has ever gone to heaven and returned. But the Son of Man has come down from heaven. And as Moses lifted up the bronze snake on a pole in the wilderness, so the Son of Man must be lifted up, so that everyone who believes in him will have eternal life.

"For this is how God loved the world: He gave his one and only Son, so that everyone who believes in him will not perish but have eternal life. God sent his Son into the world not to judge the world, but to save the world through him.

"There is no judgment against anyone who believes in him. But anyone who does not believe in him has already been judged for not believing in God's one and only Son. And the judgment is based on this fact: God's light came into the world, but people loved the darkness more than the light, for their actions were evil. All who do evil hate the light and refuse to go near it for fear their sins will be exposed. But those who do what is right come to the light so others can see that they are doing what God wants."

In the encounter with Nicodemus there is a contrast between a Pharisee who is dedicated to living by the law of Moses and the attendant laws that developed from him and Jesus, who has been performing signs and wonders that Nicodemus knows must have their origin in God. Nicodemus is curious about Jesus. Jesus is impatient with Nicodemus. We can paraphrase what Jesus tells Nicodemus like this: "You want to know how I do the things I do. The things I am doing are not part of ordinary life on this earth. They are part of God's Kingdom of eternal life, and you will not understand that Kingdom until you are born again from above." Nicodemus is confused and wants to know if Jesus is thinking he could go back to his mother's womb and be born all over again. So Jesus clarifies, "No. Human birth is human birth. I am talking about spiritual birth which is caused by the Holy Spirit. You are having a hard time understanding it because it seems mysterious. It will help you to consider our ordinary experience of the wind. You feel it blowing, but you can't explain where it came from or where it is going. You can't tie it down, but you know it's there. It's the same with God's Spirit. You can't control it, but it can fill you with God's power and bring you into a whole new reality: the Kingdom of God."

In a famous verse (John 3:16) Jesus goes on to explain why he has been sent to the earth. "For this is how God loved the world: He gave his one and only Son, so that everyone who believes in him will not perish but have eternal life. God sent his Son into the world not to judge the world, but to save the world through him." So here it is again: the key to salvation is believing in Jesus.

Yet, though God sent Jesus to save the world, there is judgment. Jesus continues: "There is no judgment against anyone who believes in him. But anyone who does not believe in him has already been judged for not believing in God's one and only Son. And the judgment is based on this fact: God's light came into the world, but people loved the darkness more than the light, for their actions were evil. All who do evil hate the light and refuse to go near it for fear their sins will be exposed. But those who do what is right come to the light so others can see that they are doing what God wants."

This is the end of the conversation. John doesn't tell us how Nicodemus responds, but later in the gospel Nicodemus quietly defends Jesus to other Pharisees who want to arrest him (John 7:50-52). Then after Jesus has been crucified, Nicodemus brings myrrh and aloes and helps prepare Jesus' body for burial (John 19: 39-40).

Judgment in the Gospel of John

The importance of recognizing and believing in Jesus as the key to entering God's domain and receiving eternal life is recorded by John in Jesus' conversation with Nicodemus. And God's judgment on anyone who fails to believe in Jesus is also explained when Jesus says that God's light came into the world, but people loved the darkness more than the light because their deeds were evil. This understanding of God's judgment is made even clearer at the very end of Chapter 3 when John tells of the reaction of John the Baptist to the news that people are flocking to Jesus instead of coming to him. Far from being jealous, John the Baptist is pleased, and this is what he says (John 3:31-36):

"The one who comes from above is above all; the one who is of the earth belongs to the earth and speaks about earthly things. The one who comes from heaven is above all. He testifies to what he has seen and heard, yet no one accepts his testimony. Whoever has accepted his testimony has certified this, that God is true. He whom God has sent speaks the words of God, for he gives the Spirit without measure. The Father loves the Son and has placed all things in his hands. Whoever believes in the Son has eternal life; whoever disobeys the Son will not see life but must endure God's wrath."

We see John's whole perspective on who Jesus is and how judgment works in chapter 3. It is a clash of realms. On the one hand is the earthly realm that John the Baptist embodies and tells us about (John 3: 31-32). On the other is the heavenly realm that Jesus belongs to, has come from, and will return to after being lifted up on the cross and calling all people to himself. When earthly people enter this realm – the realm of eternal life – they become citizens of heaven, and they will not perish but already have eternal life. When earthly people run from the opportunity to enter the realm of heaven it is because they prefer the darkness to the light. When they remain in darkness, they separate themselves from God and are subject to God's judgment and wrath (John 3: 36). The whole key is recognition. Do humans recognize Jesus as God's Messiah, or not? Do they believe in him, or not?

But then what does it mean to believe? It means this in the words of Jesus: "All who do evil hate the light and refuse to go near it for fear their sins will be exposed. But those who do what is right come to the light so others can see that they are doing what God wants (John 3:20-21)." [The Scholars Version translation puts this sentence: "But those who do what is true come into the light so the nature of their deeds will become evident: their deeds belong to God."]

Please note that "believing" in Jesus is not mere intellectual assent. As we noted earlier, an old sermon illustration points out that we can believe that the planet Saturn has rings, but that belief means almost nothing for our everyday lives. We make no decisions based on it. It creates no goals for us to achieve, not even minor ones. And there are no consequences for deciding not to believe.

In the same way, if we "believe" that Jesus is the Messiah like we believe Saturn has rings, it has no impact on us. When John speaks of "believing" in Jesus he means that we trust that Jesus has been sent by God and is the key to the most important thing in our life, which is entering God's Kingdom of Heaven. Falling in love with Jesus and walking with him through each hour of our day so that we live out his will for us and try our best to share his love with everyone is much closer to what John is saying here. When we believe in Jesus in this way, the deeds we do will be worthy of being seen in the light.

In fact, Jesus promises his disciples that after his death and resurrection he will empower them to they do even greater works than he has done in his earthly ministry. At the Last Supper, Jesus offers words of farewell to his disciples and during this Philip asks Jesus to show them the Father. Here is Jesus' response (John 14:9b-14):

"Anyone who has seen me has seen the Father! So why are you asking me to show him to you? Don't you believe that I am in the Father and the Father is in me? The words I speak are not my own, but my Father who lives in me does his work through me. Just believe that I am in the Father and the Father is in me. Or at least believe because of the work you have seen me do. I tell you the truth, anyone who believes in me will do the same works I have done, and even greater works, because I am going to be with the Father. You can ask for anything in my name, and I will do it, so that the Son can bring glory to the Father. Yes, ask me for anything in my name, and I will do it!"

Clearly, Jesus intends his followers to continue his ministry of inviting others to believe in him and doing the works that are the signs of God's love for the world. Belief is not a passive thing. True belief in Jesus becomes the center of our lives and the motive and power to carry on his works of love for those who are most in need becomes our main goal in life.

We will take a closer look at this in Chapters Seven and Eight when we take up the question of what are the signs that we have entered God's realm of eternal life even while we are living on earth – and conversely, what are the signs that we are walking on the highway to hell in this life.

Reflection Questions

1. What is your response to John's picture of Jesus being with God from the beginning of time and being the authoritative word that God spoke to call everything into existence?

2. How do you feel when you read that God sent Jesus to a people who were created through him, only to discover that they did not recognize him?

3. How did Frederica Matthewes Green's account of her faith experience strike you? Do you feel that Jesus has been at the center of your life all along and that he knows you better than you know yourself? Please write about your experience of getting to know Jesus?

4. Jesus' encounter with Nicodemus portrays a Jewish leader sincerely trying to understand who Jesus is. How do you imagine Nicodemus coming away from the conversation? Do you think Nicodemus is able to understand what Jesus is saying to him?

5. Jesus tells Nicodemus that he must be "born again" or "sired from above" -- the Greek words that John uses can mean either thing – and perhaps imply both. How does this fit with your spiritual experience? If you were to write a letter to a young person just starting to learn about Jesus, what would you say about your experience of being born again or sired from above?

6. In John 3:16 Jesus tells Nicodemus (and us) that God sent him into the world to save the world and in verse 18a Jesus says that there is no judgment for anyone who believes in him. However, Jesus goes on to say, "But anyone who does not believe in him has already been judged for not believing in God's one and only Son. And the judgment is based on this fact: God's light came into the

world, but people loved the darkness more than the light, for their actions were evil. All who do evil hate the light and refuse to go near it for fear their sins will be exposed. But those who do what is right come to the light so others can see that they are doing what God wants (John 3:18b-21)." How do you feel about this basis for God's judgment? If it is applied to you personally, what will happen?

7. How do you understand what it means to believe in Jesus? If a person believes in Jesus the same way they believe that Saturn has rings, is that enough for them to escape a damning judgment?

8. How does the promise that we can enter God's Kingdom of Heaven in this life as well as when we die feel to you? Do you already have an experience of God's eternal realm? If so, please describe it.

9. Jesus promises his followers that with his spiritual help they will do even greater things than he did during his earthly ministry. What things are you involved in doing with the spiritual help of Jesus? How do you see them as works that are full of Jesus' light?

3

Judgment and the New Testament

For Christians the words of Jesus, himself, are the first place we look to understand what judgment and hell mean to us. And as we would expect, Jesus' words are authoritative for the rest of the New Testament as well.

The Apostle Paul

Let's begin with the letters of the Apostle Paul who, like John, does not include descriptions of hell as a fiery place of torment, but who has a definite sense of God's judgment and the consequences of refusing to follow Jesus and acting in sinful ways. Paul, of course, was once a Pharisee who found the claim that Jesus was God's son completely unacceptable. At that time, his name was Saul, and he was well known for persecuting members of the new Christian church, which was forming in the years immediately following Christ' death and resurrection. Saul was on his way to Damascus with letters from the high priest in Jerusalem which would allow him to arrest Christians there. Just outside the gates, however, he had a spiritual experience in which he was knocked to the ground by a blinding light and then saw a vision of the risen Christ who said to him, "Saul, Saul why are you persecuting me?" Saul remained blind for three days and had to be helped into Damascus. Finally, a new Christian named Ananias was guided by a dream to go to Saul and pray with him to heal his blindness. From then on Saul changed his name to Paul and quickly became one of Jesus' greatest followers and the founder of many churches. Paul taught both what he was told about Jesus from the disciples who knew and followed Jesus, and from his personal experience of his new life of faith in Jesus. Some of his letters are the earliest books of the New Testament.

For Paul the Hebrew law, which he knew backwards and forwards, was good in that it taught humans right from wrong. However, Paul found that by itself, the law gave no power to actually do right. Therefore, Paul writes that the law left us in a state of separation from God, which is what the Bible means by sin. As Paul wrote in his letter to the Romans, chapter five, Adam is the father of all humans, yet because Adam sinned, he was forced out of the Garden of Eden and he eventually died. So, too, all his descendants died in a state of sin. However, at just the right time, God sent Jesus to save us from the power of sin. Jesus died on the cross, receiving the punishment that we should have received for our sins, and he opened a new way of faith in Christ that could bring us into a right relationship with God. According to Paul, when we choose to truly follow Jesus, we die with Jesus to our sins and are reborn like him into life powered by the Holy Spirit. The Spirit saves us from the temptation to sin, and gives us new life, meaning, purpose, and power so that we can live united with God and receive the same eternal life that Jesus received. For Paul, separation from God leads to condemnation and eternal death. Faith in Jesus leads to being united with God by the Holy Spirit so that we receive God's love and eternal life. (See Romans 4-8)

In Romans 6:20-23 Paul sums up his understanding and experience of how salvation and judgment now work since God has sent Jesus to show God's love for us and to die on the cross receiving the just punishment due for our sins. Here is what he writes:

"When you were slaves to sin, you were free from the obligation to do right. And what was the result? You are now ashamed of the things you used to do, things that end in eternal doom. But now you are free from the power of sin and have become slaves of God. Now you do those things that lead to holiness and result in eternal life. For the wages of sin is death, but the free gift of God is eternal life through Christ Jesus our Lord."

In Romans 8:1-9 Paul comes back to his understanding of what God did in the life and ministry of Jesus. Once again, he writes about the inability of the law of Moses to save us, about Jesus' sacrificial death, and about how faith in Jesus brings about a new life that is powered by God's Holy Spirit. Let us read it to fully understand Paul's theology:

"So now there is no condemnation for those who belong to Christ Jesus. And because you belong to him, the power of the life-giving Spirit has freed you from the power of sin that leads to death. The law of Moses was unable to save us because of the weakness of our sinful nature. So God did what the law could not do. He sent his own Son in a body like the bodies we sinners have. And in that body God declared an end to sin's control over us by giving his Son as a sacrifice for our sins. He did this so that the just requirement of the law would be fully satisfied for us, who no longer follow our sinful nature but instead follow the Spirit.

"Those who are dominated by the sinful nature think about sinful things, but those who are controlled by the Holy Spirit think about things that please the Spirit. So letting your sinful nature control your mind leads to death. But letting the Spirit control your mind leads to life and peace. For the sinful nature is always hostile to God. It never did obey God's laws, and it never will. That's why those who are still under the control of their sinful nature can never please God.

"But you are not controlled by your sinful nature. You are controlled by the Spirit if you have the Spirit of God living in you. And remember that those who do not have the Spirit of Christ living in them do not belong to him at all."

Paul also gives us specific information about the change in us that the presence of God's Spirit enables. In First Corinthians, chapter 12, Paul writes about the different spiritual gifts that God gives to members of Christ's church. He uses the example of a human body which requires many parts in order to function – hands and feet and eyes and ears and so on. He notes that no matter how important a part is, it can't live on its own without the other parts. In just this way God's Spirit empowers different spiritual gifts in different members, so that working together they will make the body of the church strong. In First Corinthians 12: 27-30 he sums it up:

"All of you together are Christ's body, and each of you is a part of it. Here are some of the parts God has appointed for the church:

"first are apostles,

second are prophets,

third are teachers,

then those who do miracles,

those who have the gift of healing,

those who can help others,

those who have the gift of leadership,

those who speak in unknown languages.

"Are we all apostles? Are we all prophets? Are we all teachers? Do we all have the power to do miracles? Do we all have the gift of healing? Do we all have the ability to speak in unknown languages? Do we all have the ability to interpret unknown languages? Of course not!"

So no person has all the gifts, but each person is given at least one gift. And then Paul famously turns to the single most important gift which lies behind and gives direction to them all: the gift of love. Love is the greatest spiritual gift and God gives it to all who have faith in Christ. Let's read First Corinthians 13:1-7:

"If I could speak all the languages of earth and of angels, but didn't love others, I would only be a noisy gong or a clanging cymbal. If I had the gift of prophecy, and if I understood all of God's secret plans and possessed all knowledge, and if I had such faith that I could move mountains, but didn't love others, I would be nothing. If I gave everything I have to the poor and even sacrificed my body, I could boast about it; but if I didn't love others, I would have gained nothing.

"Love is patient and kind. Love is not jealous or boastful or proud or rude. It does not demand its own way. It is not irritable, and it keeps no record of being wronged. It does not rejoice about injustice but rejoices whenever the truth wins out. Love never gives up, never loses faith, is always hopeful, and endures through every circumstance."

For Paul, when we are truly joined to God in Christ, love will be the driving force of our lives. And that love is eternal. Other things will fade away or lose their importance. But love will remain. Let's read the rest of chapter 13, verses 8-13:

"Prophecy and speaking in unknown languages and special knowledge will become useless. But love will last forever! Now our knowledge is partial and incomplete, and even the gift of prophecy reveals only part of the whole picture! But when the time of perfection comes, these partial things will become useless.

"When I was a child, I spoke and thought and reasoned as a child. But when I grew up, I put away childish things. Now we see things imperfectly, like puzzling reflections in a mirror, but then we will see everything with perfect clarity. All that I know now is partial and incomplete, but then I will know everything completely, just as God now knows me completely.

"Three things will last forever—faith, hope, and love—and the greatest of these is love."

As we consider what the marks of true faith in Jesus really are – and conversely, what leads to judgment and condemnation – let us keep these words about the primacy of love at the top of our minds.

The Book of Revelation

The final book of the New Testament is the Book of Revelation. And it does have descriptions of hell as a fiery place of eternal punishment. In Revelation the author, John of Patmos, tells of his dramatic vision of the last days in which there are two final resurrections that encompass all humans who have ever lived and two judgments. In the first resurrection, the souls of Christian martyrs are raised to reign with

Christ, while Satan is seized by an angel, bound in chains, and locked away in a bottomless pit for a thousand years.

After a thousand years, Satan is freed from imprisonment, raises a great army and surrounds the city of God. However, before he can harm the city, fire comes down from heaven and consumes the army. Then John tells us in Revelation 20:10 that: "Then the devil, who had deceived them, was thrown into the fiery lake of burning sulfur, joining the beast and the false prophet. There they will be tormented day and night forever and ever."

Then comes a final resurrection and final judgment. Reading from Revelation 20:11-21:1-8 we find:

"And I saw a great white throne and the one sitting on it. The earth and sky fled from his presence, but they found no place to hide. I saw the dead, both great and small, standing before God's throne. And the books were opened, including the Book of Life. And the dead were judged according to what they had done, as recorded in the books. The sea gave up its dead, and death and the grave gave up their dead. And all were judged according to their deeds. Then death and the grave were thrown into the lake of fire. This lake of fire is the second death. And anyone whose name was not found recorded in the Book of Life was thrown into the lake of fire.

"Then I saw a new heaven and a new earth, for the old heaven and the old earth had disappeared. And the sea was also gone. And I saw the holy city, the new Jerusalem, coming down from God out of heaven like a bride beautifully dressed for her husband.

"I heard a loud shout from the throne, saying, 'Look, God's home is now among his people! He will live with them, and they will be his people. God himself will be with them. He will wipe every tear from their eyes, and there will be no more death or sorrow or crying or pain. All these things are gone forever.'

"And the one sitting on the throne said, 'Look, I am making everything new!' And then he said to me, 'Write this down, for what I tell you is trustworthy and true.' And he also said, 'It is finished! I am the Alpha and the Omega—the Beginning and the End. To all who are thirsty I will give freely from the springs of the water of life. All who are victorious will inherit all these blessings, and I will be their God, and they will be my children.'

" 'But cowards, unbelievers, the corrupt, murderers, the immoral, those who practice witchcraft, idol worshipers, and all liars—their fate is in the fiery lake of burning sulfur. This is the second death.' "

Here, let us take special note of two things. First the description of hell as a lake of fire where there is torment day and night forever.

Second, the final judgment is a judgment based on deeds. The righteous are given eternal life in the holy city of the New Jerusalem. However, cowards, unbelievers, those who are corrupt, murderers, those who are immoral, those who practice witchcraft or worship idols, and all liars – they will be cast into the fiery lake of burning sulfur.

Reflection Questions

1. How does Paul's experience of seeing and hearing the risen Christ resonate with you? How is it that you experience Christ's presence accompanying you in your life? Do you feel driven to do Christ's work in any way that is near to Paul's experience of changing from persecuting the church to becoming the foremost builder of new churches? If you do not feel driven by Christ to do work he wants you to do, what do you think that means?

2. Before Paul encountered the risen Christ, Paul felt that living a life of faith meant obeying the Hebrew laws that began with the Ten Commandments of Moses and then developed as more specificity was required by particular situations. The problem with this, as Paul experienced it, was that knowing the right thing to do and having the ability to do it in the face of temptation proved to be two different things. The immense difference Jesus created was that by his faith in Jesus, Paul received the power of God's Holy Spirit taking over his human will and giving him strength to do things he was never able to do before. How do you sense God's Holy Spirit empowering you?

3. In First Corinthians 12, Paul writes that the Holy Spirit gives different spiritual gifts to different members of the church so that, working together, the members will be able to make the church thrive. What are some of the spiritual gifts that you see being given to others who are close to you? What spiritual gifts do you believe you have received?

4. In First Corinthians 13, Paul writes that all spiritual gifts must be used in love – that without love they amount to nothing. How, specifically, are you using your gifts to do Christ's works of love? Where would a non-biased observer who watched you carefully

see you doing unloving things? How much of your life do these unloving things take up?

5. Paul does not write about sinful people being sent to hell. He does, however, write about being judged by God and receiving eternal death. In Romans 6:23 Paul sums up his belief, writing, "For the wages of sin is death, but the free gift of God is eternal life through Christ Jesus our Lord." Do you believe this summary applies to you? Why or why not?

6. The Book of Revelation tells of a final judgment for all humanity which tells of eternal torment in a lake of fire for those whose deeds in life were evil. Those who are sent to hell include "cowards, unbelievers, the corrupt, murderers, the immoral, those who practice witchcraft, idol worshipers, and all liars". (Revelation 21:8) Do you accept this as part of the inerrant word of God which God speaks to us to steer us in the right direction in Life?

7. Jesus promises his followers that with his spiritual help they will do even greater things than he did during his earthly ministry. What things are you involved in doing with the spiritual help of Jesus? How do you see them as works that are full of Jesus' light?

4

Living in Relationship to God

Christians are part of a Judeo-Christian tradition that goes back in time many years before the birth of Jesus. The first people in the Bible who can be pinpointed in historical time are Abraham and Sarah, who lived about two thousand years before Jesus was born. Therefore, our Bible is divided into an Old Testament (or Hebrew Scriptures) which covers the time between Creation and the birth of Christ -- and the New Testament (or Christian Scriptures) which covers the birth and ministry of Jesus, his death and resurrection, and the formation of the first Christian churches.

During the period of the Old Testament, Abraham and Sarah become the first historical people to worship Yahweh. Somewhere between 1,450 and 1,250 years before Jesus is born (scholars disagree), the Hebrew people gradually form into a nation when Moses leads them out of slavery in Egypt and, after forty years of wandering in the wilderness, Joshua leads them across the Jordan River. During all this time – and continuing to this day – the people live in a covenant relationship with God. A covenant is an agreement between two parties that defines each party's responsibilities to the other. In this case, the Hebrew people believe that it is God's responsibility to guide and protect them as God forms them into a great nation. They also agree that it is their responsibility to seek to know God's expectations and obey them. The Ten Commandments that Moses brings down from his meeting with God on the top of Mount Sinai are laws that define God's expectations for God's people. The people believe that if they follow these laws, then

God will guide them and bless them so that they will prosper. If they fall away and do not follow them, then God will judge them and perhaps punish them by sending them some misfortune or by allowing other nations to dominate them. If the people feel they have been obedient, but God is not helping them enough or protecting them, they can plead for God's help as we find in a number of Psalms.

God Is the Highest Authority

A critical point here is that even before the birth and ministry of Jesus, God's people know that the highest authority under which they live is not a human leader or a government -- but is God. In the end, the One who holds them responsible to live in just ways is God. This fact is very important in our time of the enormous influence of media and misinformation. Politicians, churches and denominations, businesses, other nations – all have become very sophisticated at using media to influence our thinking. Media influencers push a particular viewpoint, others fall into place behind them, and in the blink of an eye they make a particular viewpoint so convincing that it is hard to tell what is true and what is false.

Yet as the Old Testament prophet Isaiah reminds us in chapter 55:8-9:

"My thoughts are nothing like your thoughts," says the Lord.
　"And my ways are far beyond anything you could imagine.
"For just as the heavens are higher than the earth,
　so my ways are higher than your ways
　and my thoughts higher than your thoughts."

There is nothing to suggest that humans are wiser now than in Isaiah's time. Or that we have anything close to the intelligence of God. The truth is that we are more confused by the swirling facts and lies that envelop us than the people of Isaiah's time. We are less able than ever to see the truth. And God's ways far exceed ours. We must tread carefully because we are on dangerous ground. And we must remember that in the end, Jesus will be our judge. The viewpoint of a president, or a news channel, or a media personality – either on the right or on the left – will not stand. As the Hebrew people always believed, God's judgment and power will prevail.

The People Want a King

From the time of Abraham and Sarah to the preaching of John the Baptist, the fortunes of God's people rise and fall according to the level of their faith in God and their obedience to God's ways. When the people are united in faith, they do well even though they are a small nation without much settled ground. When they worship other gods or fail to live justly with each other, they weaken their society and fall victim to the power of other nations such as the Philistines. About a thousand years before the birth of Jesus, they decide that they want a human king to lead them. Other nations have a king, and they think it will strengthen them. So they ask their aging leader, Samuel, to find them a king. Samuel is a very distinguished leader who was once Israel's main judge, deciding disputes that arose among the people. Now he is old, and two of his sons have taken his place. However, his sons are corrupt, and the people do not trust them. The nations around them have kings and they think a king will strengthen Israel. Samuel thinks this is a terrible idea, since they will no longer be ruled directly by God. But in a fascinating conversation God tells Samuel what to do. First, God explains the situation to Samuel in 1 Samuel 8:6-9:

"Samuel was displeased with their request and went to the Lord for guidance. "Do everything they say to you," the Lord replied, "for they are rejecting me, not you. They don't want me to be their king any longer. Ever since I brought them from Egypt they have continually abandoned me and followed other gods. And now they are giving you the same treatment. Do as they ask, but solemnly warn them about the way a king will reign over them."

So Samuel gives in to the people's plea. But first he tells them quite directly what will happen. Let's look at 1 Samuel 8:10-18:

"This is how a king will reign over you," Samuel said. "The king will draft your sons and assign them to his chariots and his charioteers, making them run before his chariots. Some will be generals and captains in his army, some will be forced to plow in his fields and harvest his crops, and some will make his weapons and chariot equipment. The king will take your daughters from you and force them to cook and bake and make perfumes for him. He will take away the best of your fields and vineyards and olive groves and give them to his own officials. He will take a tenth of your grain and your grape harvest and distribute it among his officers and attendants. He will take your male and female slaves and demand the finest of your cattle and donkeys for his own use. He will demand a tenth of your flocks, and you will be his slaves. When that day comes, you will beg for relief from this king you are demanding, but then the Lord will not help you."

Despite his warning, Israel chooses to have a king and Samuel appoints Saul – an obvious choice since Saul is tall and strong and looks the part. However, things don't go so well. The Philistines oppress the Israelites and eventually send their champion, a giant warrior named Goliath, to challenge the Israelites to a duel. They can send whoever they want to fight Goliath and whichever warrior kills the other will win the day for his side. Saul is not up to this. As you probably learned in Sunday School, a young shepherd named David takes the challenge and kills Goliath with a single stone slung from his sling. Soon David replaces Saul as king and the nation has some of its best years under him. David is a great general and a shrewd politician, but he is far from perfect. One of his sons, Solomon, replaces him when he dies and builds a great temple in Jerusalem. He also expands Israel's boundaries to the greatest extent it enjoys. But after Solomon, the nation divides into a northern part, Israel, and a southern part, Judah. As time goes on both parts are conquered. Israel by Assyria in 722 BCE and Judah by Babylonia in 586 BCE. It looks like the people are doomed. Eventually God intervenes on their behalf and a Persian King named Cyrus conquers Babylonia. Cyrus allows the Jews held captive in Babylon to leave and rebuild Jerusalem. During all this time the people begin to look for a leader from David's line who will restore the nation. And many long for justice to return to the land.

The Role of Prophets

At this point we need to remember the role of prophets. Before Israel had kings, it had judges who would decide disputes interpreting the law as it had developed from the original Ten Commandments. It also had prophets who felt a strong connection to Yahweh such that they could speak out what God was saying to them. The prophets addressed how God felt the people had broken the covenant and told what God saw as the result of their faithlessness. Often what the prophets said was offensive to people with power and as the nation began to be ruled by kings, the prophets faced strong risks in speaking out. Nevertheless, they persisted. Many of the books of the Old Testament are written by prophets and record God's words.

The Prophet Isaiah and God's Desires for God's People

One of the major prophets in the Old Testament is Isaiah. Let's look at a famous passage from Isaiah that will help us to see what he said and to connect his message to Jesus.

Here is Isaiah 58:1-12:

"Shout with the voice of a trumpet blast.
    Shout aloud! Don't be timid.
Tell my people Israel of their sins!
    Yet they act so pious!
They come to the Temple every day
    and seem delighted to learn all about me.
They act like a righteous nation
    that would never abandon the laws of its God.
They ask me to take action on their behalf,

pretending they want to be near me.
'We have fasted before you!' they say.
    'Why aren't you impressed?
We have been very hard on ourselves,
    and you don't even notice it!'
"I will tell you why!" I respond.
    "It's because you are fasting to please yourselves.
Even while you fast,
    you keep oppressing your workers.
What good is fasting
    when you keep on fighting and quarreling?
This kind of fasting
    will never get you anywhere with me.
You humble yourselves
    by going through the motions of penance,
bowing your heads
    like reeds bending in the wind.
You dress in burlap
    and cover yourselves with ashes.
Is this what you call fasting?
    Do you really think this will please the Lord?
"No, this is the kind of fasting I want:
Free those who are wrongly imprisoned;
    lighten the burden of those who work for you.
Let the oppressed go free,
    and remove the chains that bind people.
Share your food with the hungry,
    and give shelter to the homeless.
Give clothes to those who need them,
    and do not hide from relatives who need your help.
"Then your salvation will come like the dawn,
    and your wounds will quickly heal.
Your godliness will lead you forward,

and the glory of the Lord will protect you from behind.
Then when you call, the Lord will answer.
     'Yes, I am here,' he will quickly reply.
"Remove the heavy yoke of oppression.
     Stop pointing your finger and spreading vicious rumors!
Feed the hungry,
     and help those in trouble.
Then your light will shine out from the darkness,
     and the darkness around you will be as bright as noon.
The Lord will guide you continually,
     giving you water when you are dry
     and restoring your strength.
You will be like a well-watered garden,
     like an ever-flowing spring.
Some of you will rebuild the deserted ruins of your cities.
     Then you will be known as a rebuilder of walls
     and a restorer of homes.

Four things jump out at us here.

First, God is in charge. God is in charge of the entire universe. And God is in charge of the fortunes of God's people. When we read this passage, it is God's voice that we hear, not Isaiah's. Isaiah quotes what he hears from God.

Second, God is interested in the true conditions of life for God's people. God does not care how often their leaders worship, or if they fast, or if they put on sackcloth and ashes. God's concern is how those who are most in need are being treated.

Third, God is very specific. God wants workers to be treated fairly. God wants all the unfair rules which oppress people to be removed. God wants prisoners who are unfairly held to be freed. God wants all hungry people to be fed and all homeless people to be housed. God wants people in need of clothing to be given clothes and wants people to stop ignoring their own relatives when they ask for help.

Fourth, when these things are done, then God promises to answer Israel's call for help. Then and only then can the people thrive. The nation will be back on firm ground, with God watching over it and even helping people to rebuild their cities which have been destroyed.

We saw earlier in this chapter that we have a hard time today in the United States telling the truth from lies. In the chapter naming the bad things that Donald Trump and his administration are doing, we will look closely at his prodigious lies. For now, however, let's consider that our capitalistic society wants us to buy as many things as possible to drive the economy. So we are besieged by commercials urging us to buy this or that so that we will enjoy life, be attractive to others, consume great experiences like vacations to special places, avoid aging or at least looking like we are aging, etc. The unspoken idea here is that the goal of our lives should be to please ourselves. If we can look better, go on wonderful trips and eat great food, enjoy playing sports or supporting our favorite team, gamble our money and win, etc., then we will succeed at life.

Yet according to the Bible, this is decidedly not how God will judge the success of our lives! Nonetheless we see churches selling themselves in the same way. Come worship with us because we will guarantee your salvation, or we have a great Sunday School, or because our sanctuary is air conditioned, or we have a great choir, or our preacher is inspirational, etc. It then becomes all about what the church will provide for you. Prosperity preachers like Joel Osteen make a gospel of their own out of the idea that God wants you to become rich and if you just support them, they will lead you to receive a financial blessing from God.

If we fall into the trap of American consumerism, it's an easy step to assume that God's purpose is to provide for you. That God wants to make you rich or famous or healthy or a dominant leader in industry or government or Christianity. Faith then becomes all about you and what God will do for you to make you safe and happy.

Can you see that this is NOT the Bible, but American consumerism tugging at you? It is not the Spirit of God. If you truly believe the Bible, you will see that God expects you to be serving God – first and foremost by serving others. God loves you -- but not by being your Amazon in the Sky.

The best way of thinking about this is that God does not take marching orders from us. We take marching orders from God. At the minimum, God expects us to love our neighbors at least as much as we love ourselves – and if we follow the example of Jesus, then we will love our neighbors more and make sacrifices to help them.

Reflection Questions

1. Do you understand the idea of living in a covenant relationship with God, where God makes promises to God's people and the people make promises to God? Do you feel like you personally participate in this covenant? What has been the result?

2. How do you feel about Isaiah's prophecy in Isaiah 58? Isaiah is speaking God's words about how God wants the leaders of the nation to take care of the poor. Isaiah is very specific. Have you applied these words to your estimation of how the United States should be treating the poor? Do you think that God will hold you answerable for either supporting or not supporting the moral values God wants upheld? Why?

3. Do you see God as existing to help you get what you want? Or do you see yourself as existing because God created you to serve God and care for the earth and your neighbors according to the life and teachings of Jesus?

4. Do you see Jesus as the ultimate judge of truth and of human behavior? Are all people answerable to God according to Biblical standards? If we are answerable to God, what is the best way to act given the state of our nation and world?

5. What do you think of the nation of Israel wanting a king? How does Samuel's caution strike you? Are there parallels between then and now?

5

The Day of God's Judgement

As we have already seen, the Bible teaches that God, through Jesus, will judge the living and the dead and that each of us will go either to heaven and a place of eternal life and light – or to hell or a place of eternal death and darkness. In fact, God's judgment of human beings resulting in divine consequences is pervasive throughout both the Old and New Testaments. To give just a few examples, in the Old Testament:

- Psalm 9:7-8 – The Lord reigns forever, executing judgment from his throne. He will judge the world with justice and rule the nations with fairness.
- Ecclesiastes 12:14 – God will judge us for everything we do, including every secret thing, whether good or bad.
- Psalm 76:8-9 – From heaven you sentenced your enemies; the earth trembled and stood silent before you. You stand up to judge those who do evil, O God, and to rescue the oppressed of the earth.
- Isaiah 66:16 – The Lord will punish the world by fire and by his sword. He will judge the earth, and many will be killed by him.
- Micah 4:3 – The Lord will mediate between peoples and will settle disputes between strong nations far away. They will hammer their swords into plowshares and their spears into pruning hooks. Nation will no longer fight against nation, nor train for war anymore.

- Deuteronomy 32:4 – He is the Rock; his deeds are perfect. Everything he does is just and fair. He is a faithful God who does no wrong; how just and upright he is!

And then, in the New Testament:

- Acts 10:42 – (Peter's words) Jesus ordered us to preach everywhere and to testify that he is the one appointed by God to be the judge of all—the living and the dead.
- 2 Timothy 4:1 – I solemnly urge you in the presence of God and Christ Jesus, who will someday judge the living and the dead when he comes to set up his Kingdom.
- Matthew 25:31-33 – (words of Jesus) When the Son of Man comes in his glory, and all the angels with him, then he will sit upon his glorious throne. All the nations will be gathered in his presence, and he will separate the people as a shepherd separates the sheep from the goats. He will place the sheep at his right hand and the goats at his left.
- Revelation 20:12 – I saw the dead, both great and small, standing before God's throne. And the books were opened, including the Book of Life. And the dead were judged according to what they had done, as recorded in the books.

At this point it is completely clear that if we believe the Bible, there will come a time when we will stand before God and Jesus and be judged by Jesus for how we have lived our lives on earth. What standard will Jesus use?

Different passages in the Bible point to two possible standards. But as we look at them carefully, we discover that they really agree with each other and become one. Since every verse of the Bible is inerrant, this is just what we would expect. So, what are these two standards?

The first standard is our deeds. What have we done in the time we were given? Have we done the things that Jesus did? Have we loved and helped others? When our neighbors were hungry, thirsty, in need of clothing or shelter, strangers in the land, sick or in prison, have we helped them? Simply reread Jesus' Parable of the Sheep and the Goats in Matthew 25:31-46 and you will see a comprehensive list of what Jesus expects us to do. And this list reflects all the kinds of things that he did in his earthly life. There are no surprises here! This standard cannot be more straightforward.

The second standard comes from the Gospel of John and the Letters of Paul. It is whether or not we recognize who Jesus is and come to believe in him. In our chapter on John, we saw that even though Jesus is God's Son and is the Living Word that God uses to create the universe, the earth, and all human beings – still, many people fail to recognize him.

As John says in his Prologue (John 1:10-13): "He came into the very world he created, but the world didn't recognize him. He came to his own people, and even they rejected him. But to all who believed him and accepted him, he gave the right to become children of God. They are re-born—not with a physical birth resulting from human passion or plan, but a birth that comes from God."

A little later, in John's telling of Jesus meeting Nicodemus, we find these words of Jesus about salvation or destruction (John 3:16-21):

"For this is how God loved the world: He gave his one and only Son, so that everyone who believes in him will not perish but have eternal life. God sent his Son into the world not to judge the world, but to save the world through him.

"There is no judgment against anyone who believes in him. But anyone who does not believe in him has already been judged for not believing in God's one and only Son. And the judgment is based on this fact: God's light came into the world, but people loved the darkness more than the light, for their actions were evil. All who do evil hate the light and refuse to go near it for fear their sins will be exposed. But those who do what is right come to the light so others can see that they are doing what God wants."

So this second standard seems to be based more on belief than on deeds. At first glance it seems to say that if we believe that Jesus is God's Son, then Jesus will forgive us for whatever we might have done, and we will go to heaven. However, as Jesus continues, it becomes clear that those who do evil will hide in darkness, while those who do what is right will come to the light so that everyone can see that they are doing what God wants.

This part leads us back into harmony with the first standard of living the same way that Jesus lived. Anyone can claim to believe in Jesus. Especially those who want to cover up their deeds and hide in darkness. If they can appear to believe in Jesus, they may think they can escape judgment. Perhaps they will escape the judgment of humans. But God and Jesus know us through and through. And what works with humans will not work with them.

Jesus also talks with Nicodemus about being born again. And in John's Prologue he tells us that those who truly believe in Jesus receive a second birth – not a physical birth, but a spiritual birth which changes them. As the Apostle Paul puts it in Second Corinthians 5:17: "Anyone who belongs to Christ has become a new person. The old life is gone; a new life has begun!" This new life is a life powered by the Holy Spirit so that the person now lives and acts like Jesus lived and acted during his ministry on earth. And such a person will do the same kinds of deeds that Christ did. True belief goes hand in hand with doing the deeds of Christ. True belief opens us to seeing with Christ's eyes, thinking with his mind, feeling with his heart, and working to birth the Kingdom of God in the same ways that Jesus worked.

So, as we can see, the two standards are really one standard. Did we recognize that Jesus is God's Son sent to teach us how God wants us to live? Did we truly believe in Jesus – not just say we did but actually become born again and receive the Holy Spirit? And did we follow Jesus by allowing the Spirit to empower us to do the loving things that Jesus did? If we recognized Jesus, believed in him, lived a life empowered by the Holy Spirit, and carried on Jesus' ministry, we will enter eternal life now and go to live eternally with God in heaven when we are judged. If we did not, and lived a life that ignored the people most in need or took perverse pleasure in keeping them down, then we will receive the judgment of death and hell.

Again, this is very plain in the Bible. No amount of dodging and weaving and trying to figure a way to convince God and Jesus to excuse us is going to work. As we noted and have already seen, God does not take marching orders from us. We take marching orders from God.

In closing this chapter, it will be helpful to consider the Biblical example of Job. You may remember that Job has an entire book devoted to his story in the Old Testament. Job is one of the most devout men in the Bible. As his story unfolds, he does everything God requires, is living a blameless life, and has a model family with many children and a very prosperous flock of animals. He is a shining example of faith! Yet as the story continues, God allows Satan to torment Job to see if his faith is true, or if it is only based in the prosperity that has come to him because of the way he has lived. At this point, Job begins to suffer. At first his flocks wither, then his children die, his wife dies, and finally Job himself is stricken with pain and breaks out covered with boils. While all this happens, three friends visit Job and advise him to confess his sins and beg God for forgiveness. "You must have done something wrong to displease God," they tell him. "Repent. Perhaps God will stop punishing you."

Job refuses. In his heart, he believes he is blameless. He begins to demand to meet God face-to-face to plead his case. Finally, God appears to Job out of a whirlwind. Here is a bit of what God says to him (Job 38:1-21):

Then the Lord answered Job from the whirlwind:

"Tell me, if you know so much.
Who determined its dimensions
and stretched out the surveying line?
What supports its foundations,
and who laid its cornerstone

as the morning stars sang together
  and all the angels shouted for joy?"
    "Where were you when I laid the foundations of the earth?
    Tell me, if you know so much. Who determined its dimensions and
stretched out the surveying line?
What supports its foundations,
  and who laid its cornerstone
as the morning stars sang together
  and all the angels shouted for joy?
    "Who kept the sea inside its boundaries
  as it burst from the womb,
and as I clothed it with clouds
  and wrapped it in thick darkness?
For I locked it behind barred gates,
  limiting its shores."
    I said, "This far and no farther will you come.
Here your proud waves must stop!"
    "Have you ever commanded the morning to appear
and caused the dawn to rise in the east?
Have you made daylight spread to the ends of the earth,
to bring an end to the night's wickedness?
As the light approaches,
the earth takes shape like clay pressed beneath a seal;
it is robed in brilliant colors.
The light disturbs the wicked
and stops the arm that is raised in violence."
    "Have you explored the springs from which the seas come?
Have you explored their depths?
Do you know where the gates of death are located?
Have you seen the gates of utter gloom?
Do you realize the extent of the earth?
Tell me about it if you know!"

"Where does light come from,
and where does darkness go?
Can you take each to its home?
Do you know how to get there?
But of course you know all this!
For you were born before it was all created,
and you are so very experienced!"

This brilliant poetry goes on a long time, but finally God stops and addresses Job again (Job 40:1-2):
Then the Lord said to Job,
"Do you still want to argue with the Almighty?
You are God's critic, but do you have the answers?"

Job's eventual answer to God is this (Job 42:3, 5-6):
"You asked, 'Who is this that questions my wisdom with such ignorance?'
It is I—and I was talking about things I knew nothing about,
things far too wonderful for me...
I had only heard about you before,
but now I have seen you with my own eyes.
I take back everything I said,
and I sit in dust and ashes to show my repentance."

The lesson for us that we draw from Job's story is that if we have notions about excusing ourselves before God and Jesus and maybe talking them out of something, we are vastly underrating them both! Here I can't help but think of Donald Trump and the incessant lies which he invents unendingly as if that will make them true. This lying may work with some humans. But if he thinks it will work for a second with God and Jesus, he is in for a disastrous shock. Job – an amazingly articulate and truly faithful man -- repents in dust and ashes at his encounter with

God. According to the Bible, Donald Trump will be utterly exposed and will receive exactly what his awful deeds deserve.

The next chapter will examine Donald Trump's deeds -- but not even close to the way God will see and understand them.

Reflection Questions

1. How seriously have you reflected on the day of judgment when you will meet Jesus and God and account for the ways you have lived?

2. Do you feel you have been born again and received the Holy Spirit to empower your life? What has the Spirit guided and strengthened you to do? Is what you have done the same loving things that Jesus did?

3. How do your reflections about being judged by Jesus and God make you feel?

4. When you consider the story of Job do you see God's unfathomable brilliance, understanding, and power?

6

Trump's Hellscape

According to the Bible, Donald Trump and those who work for him and support him are actively working *against* the teachings, values, and model set by Jesus Christ.

In the summary, we saw two of the principal things that Donald Trump and his administration have done that completely contradict the values and ministry of Jesus. In this chapter, we will recall those things and then examine many more that he and his administration have done that no Bible-believing Christian can support. If you have already read and remembered the first two items from the summary, please go ahead to the third topic: Incessant Lies. Even with all these topics, our list will be far from complete. But at the chapter's end, I am convinced you will agree that Donald Trump and his followers are moving against Jesus, not with him.

A New Holocaust

In the Summary, we first noted that Donald Trump began his second term as president by working with Elon Musk to dismantle the United States Agency for International Development (USAID). In 1961 USAID was established to administer U.S. foreign aid and to promote global development. It supported humanitarian relief during famines and other disasters, and it strengthened education, health, and democratic governance in more than 100 nations. It helped to build alliances with these nations to increase America's security during the Cold War. USAID has continued to grow since the 1960s, reaching more and more people in need. Then, just two weeks into his administration, Trump and Musk put USAID "in the wood chipper" as they joked about it. As we saw in the Summary, crucial food aid to children starving in Sudan and other nations was immediately ended. Within a few days, children started dying. The abrupt end of funds put at least 14 million children at risk of losing nutritional support and lifesaving interventions in 2025. It also ended maternal and child health programs, reduced access to clean water and sanitation in schools, disrupted protection services for children vulnerable to sex trafficking and forced labor, and threatened access to healthcare for 95 million people worldwide, including access to vaccines and treatment for malaria. 177 countries are affected. A November 5, 2025, article in the New Yorker Daily by Atul Gawande estimated that already within the first year of Trump demolishing USAID, about 600,000 people, two-thirds of them children, have died as a result. Projections from the UCLA Fielding School of Public Health estimate that if U.S. AID is not refunded, it will result in more than 14 million deaths globally by 2030. This includes 4.5 million children under the age of five, or about 700,000 child deaths annually. By comparison, Adolph Hitler and his forces killed 6 million Jewish people and another 6 million others in the years between 1941 and 1945. That holocaust will be exceeded by two million people in the same amount of time if this unbelievably cruel and death-dealing decision is not reversed. If you support this, what will you say to Jesus on the day of your judgment?

Robbing the Poor to Give to the Rich
We also saw in the Summary that Trump's advocacy for and ultimate passage of the so-called "One Big Beautiful Bill Act" has the federal government taking money from the poor and giving it to the richest 1% of the population at a time when the income divide between the rich and poor is already the highest in U.S. history. Specifically: it causes cuts of $491 billion dollars from Medicare between the years 2027 to 2034. It also cuts nearly 1 trillion dollars from Medicaid over the next

ten years, causing 310,000 people to lose their health insurance. Because rural hospitals depend on Medicaid to fund treatment for so many of their patients, many rural hospitals across the nation have closed, leaving all their residents far away from a hospital. The same is true of nursing homes. Another result of the bill is that families in the bottom 10% of the population will lose about $1,600 in food aid each year between 2026 and 2034. It will also cut funding for schools and childcare programs. Meanwhile, the benefit to those in the bottom 20% of the population will be an average tax cut of $90 per year. Those in the top 1% will see their taxes lowered by between $64,000 and $90,000 a year. Jesus taught us that we cannot serve both God and money at the same time. (See Matthew 6:24 in the Sermon on the Mount) If you read Jesus' Parable of the Rich Man and Lazarus, which we looked at in chapter one, you will see how it turns out for those who serve the rich. (See Luke 16:19-31) If you believe in the Bible but still support Donald Trump and his policies of favoring the rich and taking from the poor, you are begging Jesus and God to send you to hell.

Now let's go beyond these two easily understandable ways that Donald Trump opposes the teachings of the Bible including the teachings of Jesus and consider others that in some cases require a more in-depth analysis.

Incessant Lies

A third way Donald Trump opposes Jesus is that he lies incessantly. Anything he sees in the news or that comes out as a government statistic which he doesn't like, he proclaims to be "fake news". An example is the lewd birthday card he drew and sent to his then close friend Jeffrey Epstein which he now claims was created by Democrats. A second more recent example is the whitewash President Trump and his administration immediately applied to the shooting and death of Renee Nicole Good in Minneapolis Minnesota by ICE agent John Ross on January 8, 2026. Without any investigation having time to begin at all, the president and several others announced that Ms. Good had attempted to run over Mr.

Ross and that he fired in self-defense. Subsequent videos revealed that this was not true, but the administration doubled down while making sure that local police authorities did not have the opportunity to join the FBI in a fair investigation. And not only that, seventeen days after Renee Nicole Good was killed, Border Patrol officers killed ICU nurse Alex Jeffrey Pretti. Alex was trying to help a woman the officers had pushed down when he was jumped and pinned to the ground. Alex was legally carrying a gun but never touched it. An officer pulled it away and then as he was pinned and helpless, officers fired ten shots into his back in less than five seconds. Before this horrific murder was widely seen on several videos, the Trump Administration said that Alex was a terrorist who was brandishing his gun and had come to kill as many officers as possible. Again, blatant and terrible lies.

Anything the president wants to promote – like the idea that blue cities are overrun with crime despite the fact that their crime rates are actually dropping – he repeats over and over. His supporter Steve Bannon explained this strategy in 2018 in an interview with Michael Lewis. Bannon said, ""The Democrats don't matter. The real opposition is the media. And the way to deal with them is to flood the zone with sh*t." (Apologies for the language here.) What Bannon was saying is that the way to get around the need to tell the truth is to flood the media with so much misinformation that the public can't make sense of it and grows frustrated with the media. The outcome is that a large portion of the public loses faith in the media and decides to trust only a single source of news. And this has been quite effective so that Trump supporters often only get information from Fox News or even more extreme right-wing sources. In the Gospel of John, Jesus teaches us about the character of the devil. Jesus says: "He has always hated the truth, because there is no truth in him. When he lies, it is consistent with his character; for he is a liar and the father of lies." (John 8:44b) The Washington Post newspaper tracked the total number of false or misleading claims that Donald Trump made during his first term as president. It totaled 30,573 over his four years with the number increasing each year.

Extreme Cruelty

Fourth is the extreme cruelty – especially to children – of Donald Trump's actions. Jesus was forthright when he addressed religious and government leaders who were protecting their power and not doing God's will. But he never used force, and he was never cruel. When Peter used a sword to cut off the ear of the High Priest's slave Malchus who was helping to arrest Jesus in the Garden of Gethsemane, Jesus healed his ear and went forward to the cross. He told his disciples, "Put away your sword. Those who use the sword will die by the sword." (Matthew 26:52) By contrast, Donald Trump has consistently chosen cruelty over compassion. In his first term as president, he deliberately separated migrant children, many of them infants and toddlers, from their parents, even though it is not a crime to seek asylum in the United States. His administration then failed to keep good records of who the children's parents were and where they could be located. As of mid-2025, about 1,300 remained separated with very little chance of reunification.

More recently, in the first months of his second term, the Trump administration built "Alligator Alcatraz" in the Florida Everglades, a detention center built to be notoriously cruel with prisoners living in vastly overcrowded tents, exposed to insects and the elements, with so few toilets that there was always a long line. At the same time, his administration sent migrants arrested by ICE to a terrible prison in El Salvador without due process, meaning that they had no opportunity in court to defend themselves and prove that they had a right to be in the United States. The conditions in El Salvador were terrible, including abusive beatings, and there were no limits on how long those sent there would be held. A last example is that during the middle of the night of Sunday of Labor Day in 2025, Donald Trump's administration tried to secretly fly 600 unaccompanied migrant children, who they were holding and had a legal responsibility to care for, to Guatemala. Only the quick action of a federal judge beginning at 2:30 am prevented the administration from doing so.

This treatment of children – especially migrant children and their parents – runs directly against God's will and was called out in a position statement issued by the General Board of the Wesleyan Church on November 24, 2025. A short piece of their extensive and direct statement gives the sense of what the Wesleyan Church says. Under a section entitled, "The Repeated, Action-Oriented Call of God" the writers say:

"God doesn't command love for immigrants once or twice. He commands it over thirty times in the Old Testament alone. And these commands are always paired with tangible action.

- "Do not mistreat or oppress a foreigner,..." (Exodus 22:21)
- "The foreigner residing among you must be treated as your native born" (Leviticus 19:34)
- "You are to love those who are foreigners, for you yourselves were foreigners in Egypt" (Deuteronomy 10:19)"

The Wesleyan Church statement goes on to say that love for foreigners is not just a feeling – but it is justice enacted action. It says that God commands not only individual actions, but that God is also concerned with the character of communities and the structures they create. Also, that God judges systems, not just individuals. By the Wesleyan standard and by any fair biblical measure, the Trump administration has taken a path that is completely wrong and will be judged so by God.

Militarizing U.S. Cities
Fifth, In the "One Big Beautiful Bill" there was an extremely large budget to increase Immigration and Customs Enforcement (ICE) personnel. In fact, in early 2026 total agents had more than doubled from 10,000 to 22,000 with funding growing from $10 billion to $28.7 billion, a 187% increase.

In September and October of 2025 the Trump administration surged hundreds of National Guard troops as well as Customs and Border Protection Agents and ICE agents to Chicago to conduct mass deportation raids. This action was not wanted by either Chicago Mayor, Brandon Johnson, or Illinois Governor, J.B. Pritzker, who filed lawsuits. On September 30, 2025, a military-style raid was conducted by highly armed agents rappelling from Black Hawk helicopters on a five-story, 130-unit apartment building using flash-bang grenades. Doors were broken down, and apartments were ransacked. Nearly everyone in the building, including U.S. citizens, military veterans, and children, was marched out of the building in freezing temperatures and held in zipties for hours. Federal officials announced that 37 undocumented individuals had been arrested. But a ProPublica investigation reported that zero criminal charges were filed in the months following the raid. The creation of a large federal militia – ICE – and its deployment to blue cities where ICE agents use military tactics, jump out of unmarked cars in masks, and tackle and subdue people without even knowing if they are undocumented or not, is the president's attempt to frighten and subdue American citizens. This is not how Jesus ever treated anyone.

Then, in early 2026, Trump began sending thousands of ICE agents to Minneapolis, Minnesota, another blue city, which he wanted to intimidate. "Do the people of Minneapolis really want to live in a community in which there are thousands of already convicted murderers, drug dealers and addicts, rapists, violent released and escaped prisoners, dangerous people from foreign mental institutions and insane asylums, and other deadly criminals too dangerous to even mention?" Trump posted on social media. This characterization of Minneapolis completely misrepresents the conditions people experience in their neighborhoods. Its crime rate for murders and assaults, for example, is less than half that of Memphis, Tennessee. Its murder rate decreased by 16% in both 2024 and again in 2025. In 2025 gunshot wound victims reduced by 18%.

What caused violence and trauma to the city in early 2026 was the behavior of the ICE agents the Trump administration sent to cause great harm. On January 8, 2026, ICE agent John Ross shot and killed U.

S. citizen Renee Good at point-blank range as she attempted to slowly drive her car away from him. He fired at her three times – once through the windshield and then twice more through the side window as her car was passing him. ICE agents then prevented a local doctor from coming to her aid, and then did nothing to help her until an ambulance arrived six minutes later. The FBI then locked the local Minneapolis crime investigation unit out of the investigation. As if that was not enough, Veterans Hospital ICU nurse Alex Pretti was then murdered seventeen days later by Border Patrol agents. Mr. Pretti was also a U. S. citizen.

Undermining American Children and Their Parents

Sixth, in addition to his extreme cruelty toward both international and migrant children, Donald Trump has cut support to American children. Although he worked to end the right to legal abortions and is lauded for his efforts by many Christians, it is fair to ask why, after trying to ensure that these babies are born, he worked so hard to make their lives difficult. A short list of what he has done includes: delaying or blocking funding for school meals and school safety; putting eligibility requirements on the Supplemental Nutrition Assistance Program (SNAP) in order to kick families off the program; ending help for parents attending school so they can get better jobs and support their families; slashing funding for investigating child sexual abuse and internet crimes against children – also for responding to reports of missing children – and also for juvenile violence prevention programs. Again, there are more examples.

Dividing Our Nation

Seventh is Donald Trump's efforts to divide our nation instead of unifying it. Jesus taught us that no house divided against itself can stand. In Matthew 12:25b the NLT translates it this way: "Any kingdom divided by civil war is doomed. A town or family splintered by feuding will fall apart."

Yet in defiance of Jesus' teaching that we must be united, Donald Trump has consistently selected "bad guys" to persecute, asking his followers to join him. During his first announcement that he would run for president on June 16, 2015, he said: "When Mexico sends its people, they're not sending their best. They're sending people who have lots of problems, and they're bringing those problems with them. They're bringing drugs. They're bringing crime. They're rapists. And some, I assume, are good people." Since then, he has continued in this vein literally hundreds of times in his public statements, referring to unauthorized immigrants as "migrant criminals, illegal monsters, killers, gang members, poisoning our country, and the largest invasion in the history of our country." In December 2025, Donald Trump attacked Somali people living in Minnesota, even though most are very productive people who have become citizens or attained the legal right to live here. He lied about them, saying that they committed 80% of the crimes committed in their area – a ridiculous exaggeration. And he called their home country a "Sh*thole nation". This is shocking language for the president of our nation to use publicly or even behind closed doors. It sets a terrible example for children and again tries to divide our nation instead of unifying it. In addition to migrants, Donald Trump has also singled out racial and religious minorities, gay and lesbian people, and transgender people. In mid-September 2025, he began including Democrats, saying, "I hate them, and I really believe they hate our country."

On one level, persecuting scapegoats is a middle school psychological move to shore up your own status within a group. When I was in seventh grade a new girl appeared in our school. She had long, wiry, flaming red hair that stuck way out from her head. She wore thick glasses (before the days of thin lenses) and had a hard time seeing. She was from a poor family and her mom sewed many of her clothes which were out of style. Perhaps because of her vision problems, she moved a little clumsily, and she was a bit overweight. Let's say her name was Susie -- not her true name. Almost immediately after she appeared, more popular students came up with a game. When Susie was in a school hallway going to class or stopping at her locker, nearby students would try to push other students into her. If they succeeded and someone touched her, they got "the Susies." They were then contaminated with them and the only way they could get rid of them was to chase another student down and wipe the Susies off on them. Then that person had to wipe them off on someone else. Meanwhile, everyone else who was watching laughed uproariously. Except Susie. She never said a word, kept her head down, and tried to move on to wherever she was going. The school administration never did anything to help her. She had a miserable year. Then she disappeared and we never saw her again.

I didn't play the game. I knew it was devastating to her, and it was wrong. But I was worried about my own popularity in the seventh grade, and I didn't have the guts to risk standing up for her. 67 years later, I still remember and regret it.

What I know now, of course, is that in middle school, all students are worried about whether they are popular or not. So, cliques form to offer at least a little protection against being laughed at, being persecuted, or being bullied. If you belong to a clique, you have at least a somewhat reliable circle of friends. You feel safe or at least safer. If no clique wants you, however, you are fair game.

But that is seventh grade. By adulthood, we hopefully reach a point of maturity where we feel secure about ourselves and don't need to play these games which focus on a scapegoat. By adulthood, we are hopefully able to see the humanity in every person – every person who, after all, has been created in the image of God bearing the stamp of Jesus.

However, Donald Trump has not reached maturity as an adult and continues to scapegoat people with devastating results, both for them individually, and for the values of our nation as a whole.

There is a much deeper evil level to scapegoating and dividing people into in-groups and out-groups. Scapegoating Jesus -- instead of listening to him and recognizing who he was and what he was doing on behalf of God -- is what ended up sending him to the cross. But not just Jesus. Adolph Hitler and his allies scapegoated and killed six million Jewish and gay and gypsy people during their so-called "final solution" in Nazi Germany. Here is a quote from Hitler in his autobiography Mein Kampf: "The Jew has always been a people with definite racial characteristics and never a religion. As a result, what arises from this is a tuberculosis of the peoples." Here, Hitler frames Jewish people not as fellow citizens or people of faith, but as a racial threat. They are a kind of tuberculosis – something that will infect other people and bring them down. Thus, they need to be eliminated – like killing off a germ.

Donald Trump is definitely headed in this darker, more evil, direction. Human beings are easily scared and are vulnerable to seeking safety within an in-group that is persecuting a different group and blaming them for all the problems of the day. This kind of black and white thinking will never hold up if we can take a breath and think about it logically. But if someone plays on our emotions and scares us enough, we may go along and act without thinking. It is beyond the scope of this book to offer a full analysis of the techniques Hitler and Donald Trump successfully use to psychologically manipulate people and cause them to support violence against scapegoats, but what the Trump administration is doing is very sophisticated and sustained. It has already resulted in extremely cruel treatment of migrant families while denying them due process in a court of law. And of this writing, it is being aimed at people he claims are political enemies, such as James Comey, Senator Adam Schiff, NY Attorney General Letitia James, and Senator Mark Kelly. Again, it is not biblical. It is the same kind of treatment that the religious leaders of Jesus' own religion used to isolate him, falsely charge him, and with the cooperation of the Roman authorities, crucify him as a common criminal rather than rejoice in his ministry as the Son of God.

A Slave to Money

Eighth is Donald Trump's prodigious greed and devotion to money. You may recall Jesus' teachings from the Sermon on the Mount that we cannot serve both God and money. Let's take time to remember his exact words:

"Don't store up treasures here on earth, where moths eat them and rust destroys them, and where thieves break in and steal. Store your treasures in heaven, where moths and rust cannot destroy, and thieves do not break in and steal. Wherever your treasure is, there the desires of your heart will also be." ...

"No one can serve two masters. For you will hate one and love the other; you will be devoted to one and despise the other. You cannot serve God and be enslaved to money." (Matthew 6:19-21, 24)

Now compare Jesus' teaching to Donald Trump in a campaign rally in Iowa on January 9, 2016, where Trump said:

"I like money. I'm very greedy. I'm a greedy person. I shouldn't tell you that, I'm a greedy – I've always been greedy. I love money, right? But you know what? I want to be greedy for our country. I want to be so greedy for our country. I want to take back money."

As president, Donald Trump always claims that other nations play the United States as a sucker. In 2016, he wanted European nations to pay more of the costs of NATO. And that notion appealed to voters. So, he had a reason to revel in his greed. He could appeal to their sense of being taken advantage of – their sense of being people who were cheated by others.

In fact, the broad theme Donald Trump has skillfully created is that he is the champion of the common good citizens of the United States who have given and given to others and thereby been drained themselves. Hearing him, they feel that racial minorities, or people on welfare of some sort, or migrants seeking a better life, or the poor of other nations, are stealing what is rightfully theirs. Over and over, Trump makes them feel aggrieved that others are first in the concern of the government while they are taken for granted.

Yet look at the harmful and unnecessary divisions that this creates within the citizens of our nation.

- The average American's sense of how much of their money is going to help others is wildly overblown. Polls consistently show that Americans believe the U.S. spends about 25% of the federal budget on foreign aid. The actual amount is 1.2% with about 40% of the 1.2% going to military assistance and 60% going to humanitarian aid. That means that actual spending for disaster relief, global health, food security, education, and democracy promotion is .72% of the federal budget – about ¾ of 1%. And that was before the destruction of USAID.

- The average American also believes that about 30% of the federal budget goes for welfare programs inside the United States. In fact, means-tested welfare programs for food and housing assistance make up about 16% of the federal budget.

- There is a significant return on investment when we help people in need. Studies show that every dollar spent on the Supplemental Nutrition Assistance Program (SNAP) generates $1.50-$1.80 in economic activity as recipients spend locally on food and essentials. Moreover, helping people in need allows them to get an education (think of children going to school who are not distracted by hunger or parents who can scrape together funds to take classes at a community college). Help may allow someone to recover from an injury or an illness. It may help them prepare for a better job. Federal assistance isn't just a lifeline – it's a launchpad. It gives people the breathing room to heal, learn, return to work, and contribute.

- Polls show that every year the happiest nations on earth are Denmark, Sweden, or Norway -- those with a social safety net. Their citizens see the value of community and trust that, working together, they can all achieve a higher quality of life and a deeper sense of security.

- Worst of all, Donald Trump's picture of success in life runs directly opposite Jesus. He pictures the measure of success in life to be accumulating economic wealth instead of pleasing God by putting up treasure in heaven — in other words loving our neighbors as we love ourselves. This undermines the vision of American as a place of welcome to all kinds of people – and -- unless we are full-blooded native Americans -- our nation most assuredly welcomed our ancestors from different lands.

- And Trump's vision also leads to massive corruption. Trump says that he wants to help America. But first and foremost, he helps himself! In 2024 he sold out to the oil industry to get a billion dollars for his election campaign and now he is doing everything he can to increase drilling for oil. But suppressing the expansion of clean energy directly leads to more forest fires, smoke-filled air, destroyed homes, and destructive hurricanes. His tariffs often depend on how much foreign nations will support him financially. He creates policies that help his investments such as supporting an expansion of cryptocurrency – from which he and his family have made billions since his second term as president began. He makes the government use his facilities – for example his Scottish golf course during his first term as president -- and then overcharges the government for their use. His tax policies favor the top 1% of the American population while taking money away from the bottom 20% as we have seen.

- Finally, let's remember the story of the rich young man who came to Jesus to ask what he needed to do to inherit eternal life. The gospels of Matthew, Mark, and Luke all tell it very similarly. Let's read it from Mark 10:17-25 NLT:

"As Jesus was starting out on his way to Jerusalem, a man came running up to him, knelt down, and asked, "Good Teacher, what must I do to inherit eternal life?" Why do you call me good?" Jesus asked. "Only God is truly good. But to answer your question, you know the commandments: 'You must not murder. You must not commit adultery. You must not steal. You must not testify falsely. You must not cheat anyone. Honor your father and mother.'

"Teacher," the man replied, "I've obeyed all these commandments since I was young." Looking at the man, Jesus felt genuine love for him. "There is still one thing you haven't done," he told him. "Go and sell all your possessions and give the money to the poor, and you will have treasure in heaven. Then come, follow me."

At this the man's face fell, and he went away sad, for he had many possessions. Jesus looked around and said to his disciples, "How hard it is for the rich to enter the Kingdom of God!" This amazed them. But Jesus said again, "Dear children, it is very hard to enter the Kingdom of God. In fact, it is easier for a camel to go through the eye of a needle than for a rich person to enter the Kingdom of God!"

Looking at the actions of Donald Trump, we have seen that he is a prime example of Jesus' warning.

Corrupt Leadership

Ninth, Donald Trump is an abject failure when it comes to being a servant leader in the model of Moses and Jesus – and in the model of great American presidents such as Abraham Lincoln and George Washington. As we have already seen, throughout his ministry Jesus helped the weak and those who were condemned by the leaders of his time like the Samaritan woman at the well or Zaccheus the tax collector. He healed the sick and ate with those who were considered unclean or even traitors helping the Romans. He led by inviting everyone into the Kingdom of God. He had no money. He had no fancy clothes, no great horse to ride, no trappings of wealth or power at all. He never traveled to sightsee or enjoy a vacation. He put others first. The contrast with Donald Trump could not be greater.

A true leader cares for those in need – think Moses striking the rock to give his people water or Jesus healing the sick and feeding 5,000 families. A true leader tells the truth – think Moses bringing the Ten Commandments down from Mount Sinai or Jesus telling the parables we love. A true leader has a vision of a better land in which God's Spirit truly reigns – think the promised land that Moses sees even though he, himself, will have to stay behind or the Kingdom of God that Jesus announces and then goes to after his resurrection. A true leader suffers along with the people he or she is leading – think Moses in the wilderness for forty years or Jesus arrested, tortured, and crucified. A true leader is trustworthy and doesn't sell out to better themselves – think Moses continually speaking with God to get direction and Jesus refusing the devil's offer of all the kingdoms of the world in return for Jesus worshipping him.

Some people who know that Donald Trump cannot meet any of these standards have said that, nevertheless he is God's instrument, something like King Cyrus of Persia who overthrew the Babylonian empire and then allowed the Jewish people who were captive there to return to Jerusalem and rebuild it after the Babylonians had destroyed it. But Donald Trump is not releasing Americans held in some foreign land and then forgetting about them. He is embedded here and with thousands of collaborators who work directly for him, he is trying to take over America and run it by his values in his way. And as we have seen his way directly opposes Jesus. It is evil, and it will be judged so by Jesus.

Christian Nationalism

Tenth is Donald Trump's embrace of Christian Nationalism (CN), a supposedly Christian movement to bring the government of the United States under the control of "Christian law" as it is defined in the Bible according to CN leaders.

At first glance, the name Christian Nationalism seems harmless enough. If it is good to be a Christian and good to be a patriot, then what's wrong with bringing them together? On the surface it seems good, but sometimes names cover up things that are evil and that cause great harm. Unfortunately, this is the case with CN, and in Donald Trump's second presidency we are seeing it in action.

Let's begin by asking, "What is Christian Nationalism, and what is its true purpose?" CN is a movement that aims to change the United States from a democracy to a theocracy. If successful, our nation will no longer be governed according to the Constitution of the United States by representatives elected by its citizens. Instead, a relatively few white "Christian" men will control the government and impose their will on the people.

A theocracy implies a government headed by God – but since God does not appear to us directly, the government is headed by human officials who claim to be divinely inspired by God and who follow religious laws based on the particular religious texts or doctrines that they choose as most important according to their needs. In a theocracy there is no separation of church and state. When that happens, we end up with countries like Iran, a nation with which we are currently at war as of this writing. As we see with Iran, in a theocracy, too much power is placed in the hands of too few people, and soon enough it corrupts them. The citizens lose their rights. The government represses and imprisons them. And the very few at the top grow enormously rich while the vast majority suffer poverty and growing resentment.

Yet although he has chosen to start a war with Iran, Donald Trump and his supporters are working to tear up the United States' constitution and do away with democracy. For example, U.S. Representative from Colorado Lauren Bobert, a great supporter of Donald Trump, said in a June 26, 2022, speech: "The church is supposed to direct the government. The government is not supposed to direct the church. That is not how our Founding Fathers intended it." She then went on to say, "I'm tired of this separation of church and state junk that's not in the Constitution."

In fact, the First Amendment to the Constitution says, "Congress shall make no law respecting an establishment of religion, or prohibiting the free exercise thereof..." This means there can be no state religion, and our government cannot force our citizens to practice a religion or not to practice one at all. In a letter to the Danbury Baptist Association, Founding Father Thomas Jefferson explained that the First Amendment was intended to build "a wall of separation between Church and State."

The reason that Thomas Jefferson, George Washington, James Madison, John Adams, and the other founders wanted to create that separation of church and state is that they were very aware of the devastating wars in Europe fought over religion. For example, the Thirty Years' War (1618-1648) started between Catholic and Protestant states in what is now Germany. It grew into a general European war that killed millions of people. Then there was the English Civil War (1642-1651) between Puritans and Anglicans. In this war, each side proved to be just as repressive as the other. Our Founders acted to help the United States be as unified as possible so the enormous suffering they saw in Europe would never happen here.

Christian Nationalists are apparently ignorant of our Founders' knowledge of history and common sense. Instead, they claim that the United States is intended by God to be a second "Promised Land" and has been given to white Christians – mainly protestants – to inhabit and control. To satisfy God's will, they claim God wants them to create a theocracy in which the will of the people must always be subject to Old Testament laws of the Bible so that people will live in biblical ways. Tellingly, they almost never bring up Jesus.

Since he took office a second time, Donald Trump's administration has been working to implement this authoritarian rule by following the Project 2025 plan which he falsely claimed to know nothing about prior to his election. As Trump works the plan, a relatively select few white "Christian" men are being empowered to control the government and to try to control the people. Billionaire funders of the effort want to stay in the dark, with their identities and financial support unknown, but their payoff is lower taxes, less regulation, and financially rewarding government contracts. When those who pay want to stay hidden, it is always a bad sign of collusion and corruption. Remember Jesus' words in John 3:19-21: "Judgment is based on this fact: God's light came into the world, but people loved the darkness more than the light, for their actions were evil. All who do evil hate the light and refuse to go near it for fear their sins will be exposed. But those who do what is right come to the light so others can see that they are doing what God wants."

Here are some of the evil things that the Trump administration is doing which reflect its desire to implement CN:

- Trump replaced thousands of federal workers, and many key leaders in the military. As he began his second term as president, he joined with Elon Musk to create the "Department of Government Efficiency" (DOGE) and began firing thousands of experienced federal workers. He gutted federal departments like Education, or Health, Education and Welfare, making them nonfunctional in the traditional ways they had been working and putting in people who would obey his directions.

- Trump also appointed officials in traditionally independent offices like the Department of Justice or the FBI with leaders who would do his bidding, for example, by filing charges against anyone he decided was an enemy including people he appointed to work in his first administration who later criticized him.

- Trump replaced 9 of the top generals in the military and fired or replaced the top 3 attorneys in the Judge Advocates General (JAG) corps, especially those who were Black or who were women. In each case he replaced them with officers he felt confident he could trust to do his bidding. This is because he does not want the military to question the legality of his orders. One example of how this has helped Trump accomplish an extremely cruel and probably illegal action is his use of the military to destroy what he claimed were drug boats coming from Venezuela. These small vessels were destroyed, and some defenseless civilian sailors were deliberately killed, with Trump providing no evidence that the boats had drugs aboard or that their intended purpose was to harm Americans. Trump also wants the military to do his bidding inside American cities, which the Posse Comitatus Act of 1878 forbids. To create an exception Trump must invoke the Insurrection Act of 1807 which he has not done as of this writing, but which he has threatened to do many times.

- Similarly, Trump created false reasons to nationalize and deploy National Guard troops to "blue" cities, including Los Angeles, Washington DC, and Chicago. Lawsuits filed by state attorneys general have largely succeeded in preventing him from going further as of this writing.

- In the so-called On Big Beautiful Bill, Trump passed funding to increase the budget simply for Immigration and Customs Enforcement (ICE) by 75 billion dollars over the next four years. In all,170.7 billion dollars in additional funding for all the parts of immigration and border enforcement was passed. That enormous sum of money is being used to ramp up the deportation of immigrants and refugees, with an ICE goal as of this writing that is 3,000 people per day. As we saw in Minneapolis, masked ICE and Border Patrol agents have also been used to intimidate and to create chaos in the lives of United States citizens. At the same time, the bill cut 1.4 *trillion* dollars over ten years to programs that support low-income citizens, many who are children, like Medicaid and the Supplemental Nutrition Assistance Program (SNAP).

- Trump also created a deliberate program of cruelty to immigrants and even congressional representatives who wanted to inquire into what was going on. This includes racial profiling, masked ICE agents jumping out of unmarked cars to wrestle unsuspecting people to the sidewalk and to put them into the cars to whisk them away. This separated parents from their children, denied those arrested due process before they were deported, and ended up providing inadequate or vastly delayed medical care. Many arrested were also subjected to solitary confinement, and a lack of oversight. Trump's purpose is to create fear in the immigrant community and fear on the part of anyone who protests his treatment of immigrants that the same thing will happen to them.

- Trump's administration is using private contractors who are part of the behind the scenes funding of CN to build and operate an increasingly vast private prison system to house arrested immigrants until deporting them. It is fair to ask, once the many immigrants he deports are gone, who will go into those prisons next? Perhaps U.S. citizens who are his political opponents?

- The last piece of our relatively quick look at CN is the Seven Mountain Mandate (7MM) which goes all the way back to about 1975 in the planning of conservatives. This plan mobilizes followers to "invade" the seven "spheres" or "mountains" of society: family, religion, education, media, entertainment, business, and government.

- 7MM demonstrates the large reach into every aspect of life that CN seeks to control. Adherents of the plan utilize so-called "spiritual warfare tactics," including researching and mapping the "geographical strongholds of territorial spirits," using prophecy to name demons, and engaging in intercession to cleanse locations of spiritual resistance.

Since its inception it has quietly worked to replace local school board members with its followers and to elect judges at every level who agree with its principles. More recently we have seen billionaires sympathetic to the aims of 7MM purchase large media companies like CBS, the Washington Post, and Warner Brothers, Discovery.

Participating in or backing Christian Nationalism is spiritually indefensible. The people behind it seek absolute control, which in the history of human beings has repeatedly proved to corrupt absolutely. Their tactics and treatment of those they are seeking to control is largely unloving and flies directly in the face of Jesus' life and teachings. As one further example, consider the words of Pastor Doug Wilson whose preaching is at the heart of CN: "Southern slavery was not only sanctioned by the Bible, but thanks to the patriarchal kindness of their evangelical masters, a positive, happy, and pleasant experience for the majority of southern blacks." His words are an obvious barefaced lie and an example of the lengths to which CN leaders will go to cover up their true motive of domination.

Remember that some human beings will seek absolute power and even take pleasure in causing pain to others. In most cases, people like this have been abused as children and have serious mental problems. A long list of mental health professionals and even members of Donald Trump's family have pointed out that he suffered abuse as a child, particularly from his father. The Mayo Clinic describes the condition of Antisocial Personality Disorder in this way:

Definition: A lifelong mental health condition where a person consistently shows no regard for right and wrong and ignores the rights and feelings of others.

Key Symptoms:

- Repeatedly ignoring right and wrong.
- Using charm or wit to manipulate others for personal gain.
- Feeling no guilt or remorse about harming others.
- Persistent lying, deceitfulness, and impulsivity.

It is easy to recognize that Donald Trump suffers from this serious personality disorder. It is also scary because people with this disorder are not trustworthy as leaders. Getting on their side and supporting them because we believe their lies will turn out to be an extremely harmful thing to do to our souls. Instead, we must create loving, nonviolent resistance. We do that to help our beloved nation remain a democracy. We do that to keep even more children and others in need from dying or suffering unnecessarily. And in the end, we also do that to help Donald Trump keep from piling up even more terrible crimes on his soul.

Reflection Questions

1. If you feel this might be helpful, imagine yourself sitting down with Jesus to talk about how children should be treated. What does Jesus say to you? How does Jesus feel about children being left to starve or being torn away from their parents?

2. Have you tried to advance yourself by habitually lying or going back on your word? Can Donald Trump meet the standard you have set? Can he meet Jesus' standard? How do you feel about this?

3. Are you comfortable with Donald Trump scapegoating migrants, or racial minorities, or gay and lesbian people, or his political opposition as the cause of all the problems in our nation? Do you think that eliminating them or vastly suppressing them will help? What do you think God thinks?

4. How important is money to you? Has making money been the driving force of your life? Do you think that Donald Trump may be driven by money?

5. Had you heard of Christian Nationalism before reading the quick look about it that we took at the end of this chapter? Having read about it now, or considering it again, how does supporting it make you feel?

6. How do you feel about standing hand in hand with Donald Trump at the last judgment?

7

Marks of Eternal Life

At this point in the book you may be wondering, "Which path am I really on? Am I truly walking the narrow path that leads to life and the Kingdom of Heaven? Or have I lost my way, so that I am taking that broad, more popular road that leads to eternal death and the domain of hell?" In this chapter we will look carefully at a key passage in John where Jesus tells us that eternal life is a reality that we can enter now – in this life – before we die. And then we will think together about how eternal life in the present will feel for one who is on the narrow path. At the deepest level, our goal as Christians is to be citizens of heaven even while we are living on earth.

We find the key passage we want to consider carefully in John 5:19-29. Here Jesus enters a gathering conflict with the religious leaders of his faith – Judaism -- that will lead to his crucifixion. What gets him in trouble is that he heals a man on a Sabbath day and tells him to do something that qualifies as work. As you may know, the Fourth Commandment says that God's people must not work on their day of rest. Here is the whole commandment as we find it in the Book of Exodus 20:8-11:

"Remember to observe the Sabbath day by keeping it holy. You have six days each week for your ordinary work, but the seventh day is a Sabbath day of rest dedicated to the Lord your God. On that day no one in your household may do any work. This includes you, your sons and daughters, your male and female servants, your livestock, and any foreigners living among you. For in six days the Lord made the heavens, the earth, the sea, and everything in them; but on the seventh day he rested. That is why the Lord blessed the Sabbath day and set it apart as holy."

Already by the fifth chapter in John's account, religious leaders are watching Jesus closely because they sense he is a threat to their position and power. However, Jesus goes unannounced to a festival in Jerusalem and walks by the pool of Bethesda near the Sheep Gate. It's a Sabbath day, but he finds a crippled man who has been unable to walk for 38 years. Jesus asks him if he truly wants to be healed and when the man says yes, Jesus tells him to get up, take his bedroll, and walk. And he does! Simple as that.

Yet instead of rejoicing at the miraculous healing, the religious leaders become upset that the man is breaking the Fourth Commandment by doing the work of carrying his bedroll. In the argument that follows, Jesus tells them, "My Father is working straight through, even on the Sabbath. So am I." (John 5:17) As he tells the story, John then explains how the religious leaders react to Jesus. John says: "That really set them off. The (religious leaders) were now not only out to expose him; they were out to kill him. Not only was he breaking the Sabbath, but he was calling God his own Father, putting himself on a level with God." (John 5:18) Suddenly the stakes become very high! We might expect Jesus to say something to make these leaders feel more comfortable. But instead, he levels with them in detail (John 5:19-29):

Jesus said, "I'm telling you this straight. The Son can't independently do a thing, only what he sees the Father doing. What the Father does, the Son does. The Father loves the Son and includes him in everything he is doing.

"But you haven't seen the half of it yet, for in the same way that the Father raises the dead and creates life, so does the Son. The Son gives life to anyone he chooses. Neither he nor the Father shuts anyone out. The Father handed all authority to judge over to the Son so that the Son will be honored equally with the Father. Anyone who dishonors the Son, dishonors the Father, for it was the Father's decision to put the Son in the place of honor.

"It's urgent that you listen carefully to this: Anyone here who believes what I am saying right now and aligns himself with the Father, who has in fact put me in charge, has at this very moment the real, lasting life and is no longer condemned to be an outsider. This person has taken a giant step from the world of the dead to the world of the living. (Italics here are mine.)

"It's urgent that you get this right: The time has arrived—I mean right now!—when dead men and women will hear the voice of the Son of God and, hearing, will come alive. Just as the Father has life in himself, he has conferred on the Son life in himself. And he has given him the authority, simply because he is the Son of Man, to decide and carry out matters of Judgment.

"Don't act so surprised at all this. The time is coming when everyone dead and buried will hear his voice. Those who have lived the right way will walk out into a resurrection Life; those who have lived the wrong way, into a resurrection Judgment."

Eternal Life Now

As we read – and maybe reread – Jesus' words, we see the flow of his argument. Jesus says that God has sent him on a mission. Because Jesus is God's Son, God has given him God's power to give life and God's authority to judge who can receive it. Because of this, Father and Son are inseparable. Whoever dishonors one, dishonors both. Whover honors one, must honor both. Anyone, then, who believes that Jesus is truly God's Son, who aligns themselves with God, and who puts the Son in charge of his or her life, has at that moment stepped into eternal life. They have taken a giant step from the world of the dead into the world of the living.

Three words stand out here. Believe. Align. Charge. To step into eternal life in the here and now – to become citizens of heaven -- we:

- Believe that Jesus is truly God's Son.
- Align ourselves with God.

• And put Jesus in charge of our life.

Believe

Believing that Jesus is truly God's Son means coming to see the forest from the trees. Our world – even more perhaps than when Jesus lived – is full of problems and pleasures, opportunities and fears, which call out for our attention and distract us from investing ourselves in what is truly good and what is eternal. Yet behind all the commotion, God still works to bring the Kingdom of Heaven to earth. Jesus is not physically here with us anymore. Yet as we shall see in a moment, Jesus is present with us in the Holy Spirit – or the Spirit of Christ -- and he empowers us to carry on his ministry of love.

As we saw in Chapter Two, John begins his gospel with the story of how Jesus is present with God at creation and how Jesus is the logos – or the power of things to stick together – that God uses to speak words that call the universe into being. "Let there be light!" And there is light. "Let there be a space between the waters, to separate the waters of the heavens from the waters of the earth." And sky appears. Throughout the six days of creation God speaks through Jesus, and order is created out of chaos. And God sees that everything is good. Understanding who Jesus is and how he serves his Father makes it possible for us to believe that his life and continuing spiritual presence is the key to everything truly important in our lives. This is not a casual belief, but the foundation of everything that provides meaning to our lives. It is our rock.

Align

Now, God speaks to us in the depths of our souls through the Spirit of Christ. And God creates order in our chaotic lives and sticks us together. And it is good. This is what it means to come into alignment with God.

Charge

Gradually, as we come to trust in what God is doing, we see that the loving Spirit of Christ is our constant companion and guide. We learn to listen for him in every experience and follow his lead. This is what it means to put Jesus in charge of our lives.

Have the Mind of Christ

One way of developing how we understand believing in Jesus, allowing his living Spirit to bring us into alignment with God, and finally putting Jesus in charge of our lives is to consider a principal teaching of the Apostle Paul. Paul is surely one of those who walked the narrow road that leads to eternal life. In Chapter Three, we saw how he comes to see the forest from the trees on the road to Damascus when the sight and voice of the resurrected Christ literally knocks him down and blinds him for three days until one of Christ's followers comes to pray with him, heal his blindness, and set him on the path to do Christ's ministry.

Paul, then, begins to form new Christian churches. At first, he teaches about Jesus in Jewish synagogues. But as he finds resistance there, Paul begins reaching out to Gentiles – non-Jewish people who mainly speak Greek and live in Roman territory. Many years later, near the end of his ministry, Paul becomes imprisoned in Rome and writes a letter to the church he founded in Phillipi. It is a kind of farewell letter since Paul is unsure whether he will ever see these Christians again. But he wants to leave them with some lasting advice that will keep them together over the years to come.

Let's explore what he writes to them in Philippians 1:27 (NLT) and 2:1-11 (NIV):

"Above all, you must live as citizens of heaven, conducting yourselves in a manner worthy of the Good News about Christ. Then, whether I come and see you again or only hear about you, I will know that you are standing together with one spirit and one purpose, fighting together for the faith, which is the Good News. ...

"Therefore if you have any encouragement from being united with Christ, if any comfort from his love, if any common sharing in the Spirit, if any tenderness and compassion, then make my joy complete by being like-minded, having the same love, being one in spirit and of one mind. Do nothing out of selfish ambition or vain conceit. Rather, in humility value others above yourselves, not looking to your own interests but each of you to the interests of the others.

"In your relationships with one another, *have the same mindset as Christ Jesus*:

"Who, being in very nature God,
 did not consider equality with God something to be used to his own advantage;
rather, he made himself nothing
 by taking the very nature of a servant,
 being made in human likeness.
And being found in appearance as a man,
 he humbled himself
 by becoming obedient to death—
  even death on a cross!
 Therefore God exalted him to the highest place
 and gave him the name that is above every name,
that at the name of Jesus every knee should bow,
 in heaven and on earth and under the earth,
and every tongue acknowledge that Jesus Christ is Lord,
 to the glory of God the Father."

Paul gives us a very clear and powerful picture of what it means to recognize who Jesus is and to put our faith in him. He also shows us what it means to be born again or to be sired from above as we explored in Chapter Four when we looked together at the encounter between Jesus and Nicodemus.

"Have the same mindset in you that was in Christ Jesus," Paul says. And what mindset was that exactly?

Paul reminds us that Jesus had the same nature as God. Yet instead of clinging to his divinity and protecting his position, he gave it up and made himself nothing. Then he took on a human life with all its vulnerabilities and became a servant to God's will, even obeying God to the extreme point of dying on a cross.

Jesus is the ultimate servant leader, with the emphasis on servant. And Paul says that it is that attitude of a servant that should be our mindset so that we think more highly of others than we do of ourselves and that we put the interests of others first.

Lets explore this mindset of Jesus as he performs his ministry.

First, Jesus follows his Father. "The Son can't independently do a thing, only what he sees the Father doing. What the Father does, the Son does," Jesus says. If we are on the narrow road that leads to eternal life, then this must be our mindset as well!

We have a tendency to think that we own our lives (more on this in the next chapter when we take up how it feels to be on the broad road to hell). But this is NOT what Jesus shows us. Jesus takes his marching orders from God. His mission is to bring eternal life to the world – to birth the Kingdom of Heaven right here, right now. He is not trying to make money. He is not trying to elbow out other leaders and take power. He is not planning great vacations or spending time fixing up his house. His life is a living demonstration of God's love. As St. Francis once said, "Preach the Gospel always. When necessary, use words."

God fills Jesus with the Holy Spirit at his baptism. Then everywhere he goes, the Spirit shines around him like the light of heaven. Some powerful people are afraid of that light, because it will reveal their selfish, evil deeds. But ordinary people – those Jesus names in his Beatitudes at the beginning of his Sermon on the Mount – rejoice in the light! They immediately feel God's love and are healed inside and out.

Now here's the thing. John tells us that when Christ comes to his disciples for the first time on Easter evening, following his resurrection, he tells them, "Just as the Father sent me, so now I'm sending you." Then he breathes on them the Holy Spirit (see the story in John 20:19-22). Now the same Spirit that empowers him during his ministry is in his disciples and followers. And the Spirit then sets about empowering Jesus' followers to do the same things he did. So, like him, we bring the revolutionary power of God's love into the world to give birth to the Kingdom of Heaven. And Christ's light shines in us when we love as he did. And those who recognize what that light means to them come running to it to step out of the darkness of death into life eternal! What did Jesus say?

"Anyone here who believes what I am saying right now and aligns himself with the Father, who has in fact put me in charge, has at this very moment the real, lasting life and is no longer condemned to be an outsider. This person has taken a giant step from the world of the dead to the world of the living."

This is the mindset of those on the narrow path that leads to eternal life. Their fundamental identity is to have the same mindset as Jesus and follow the guidance of his Spirit to continue his work of birthing God's Kingdom.

Do you remember Frederica Matthewes-Green's conversion experience that we explored in Chapter Two when we looked at how the Gospel of John presents Jesus' teaching about how eternal life as both a present and a future experience? In that experience she discovered that Jesus was already dwelling in her soul and that he knew her life better than she knew herself.

You and I have souls as well with roots that stretch back to the Creative Spirit of Jesus who formed human beings so that each one of us bears his stamp. Each of us has an Inner Christ who dwells deep inside us and who may or may not be known by our conscious executive egos – the psychological part of us that plans our days and tries to figure out how we can become happy. The problem, however, is none of us can avoid being hurt, sometimes in traumatic ways. When we get hurt, our conscious egos get frightened, fearful, and selfish. Then they direct us to think of ourselves first and others second – the exact opposite of what Paul teaches the Philippians.

If there is a secret to life, it is for our conscious egos to make friends with our Inner Christ, to come to trust his presence, to fall in love with him, and be directed by his living Spirit. When this happens, we learn to stop habitually making transactional, self-centered decisions that seem to be shortcuts to things that benefit us. When our Inner Christ emerges, we discover a spiritual strength and direction that are unlike anything we experienced before. For one thing, our Inner Christ is not afraid to die. Why would He be? He is already resurrected! For another thing, our Inner Christ has God's perspective on the whole of our earth and the things that make for its health and the health of all humanity.

What our Inner Christ knows is this: everything depends on God. The beauty of the earth that we enjoy, the resources to grow food and build houses, the lives of our family members and friends, the wider communities in which we live, the nations that we trade with... we could go on and on with this list. Literally everything that we have, including all the minutes that we are alive, is a gift from God. We didn't create ourselves. We didn't create the laws of nature and the way the earth is formed. We are entirely dependent on God to be able to enjoy these things.

No matter where we go or what happens to us, God is present. God's Spirit – the Spirit of Jesus – tugs on us constantly to use our time and talents in ways that will embody God's love and make our lives as rich and full as they can possibly be. This happens on a moment-to-moment basis. God's Spirit of love tugs on my heart as I write these words – and God's Spirit of love tugs on your heart as you read them.

God always gives us a choice about how we will respond to the Spirit. We can feel it and dance with it. Or our conscious egos can reject it and go our own ways. What Jesus does so superbly in his human life is to dance with God's Spirit, move with it, embody its love, and create the possibility for others to experience that love in all that he says and does.

The light of God's Spirit shines in him and gives birth to the Kingdom of Heaven.

Let's try this way of thinking about what it means to be a citizen of heaven even while we live on this earth. Have you ever thought of yourself as a minister? Have you ever imagined how it would be to live with a "Rev." in front of your name? That may seem crazy to you! If you are a man, maybe you think that makes you a sissy. Maybe you think it takes away your manhood, or that you can't enjoy a drink with your friends. If you are a woman, maybe you think it's a role you can't have. Maybe your church only ordains men.

Yet what the biblical record shows is that Jesus chose all kinds of men and women to join his band of followers. They are completely human. They make mistakes. They are afraid of the same things that we fear. They are tempted to be selfish and to hurt others if it shores up their sense of safety. They struggle to get on his wavelength, to have his mindset. But eventually they learn. And like the Apostle Paul they see into the heart of things – into the eternal nature of love that he writes about so eloquently in First Corinthians 13.

When we live guided by the Spirit of Jesus so that our Inner Christ shines out and gives birth to God's love in our world then we are on the narrow road that leads us to eternal life both in the here and now and also after we die. And that is ministry. We may not be ordained by a church, but we are ministers none the less.

To sum up. here are five biblical signs that we have stepped into real, lasting eternal life. That we are no longer condemned to be outsiders. That we have taken a giant step from the world of the dead into the world of the living.

Centered and Secured by Christ

The first sign is that we feel accompanied by the loving Spirit of Christ which walks with us every day of our lives. Christ's Spirit centers us – creates order out of the chaos that might otherwise pull us apart. Jesus felt that he and his Father were one. In the same way, we will feel that we and Jesus are one. Christ's Spirit is our rock, our ultimate source of security. When the winds of life blow and the rains beat down, the house of our lives doesn't collapse because we are built upon the rock. Christ's Spirit is eternal. Christ's Spirit tugs at our Inner Christ or soul and guides us. We are not afraid to die because we know and feel where we are going: heaven. Christ's Spirit keeps us in balance, so we don't go running in a panic after wealth or power to try to keep ourselves secure. "Put up treasures in heaven," Christ says. "For where your treasure is, there your heart will be also."

Loving

The second sign is that we are filled with Jesus' love, and that his Spirit fills us with his love for all the world. Remember his teachings? "Love one another as I have loved you." ... "Love God with all your heart and soul and mind and strength and love your neighbor as yourself." ... "Love your enemies and pray for those who persecute you." We will not hate anyone, even people who oppress us. We will not be filled with fear for our safety. We will not be manipulated by leaders who know we are afraid and then play on our fears to advance themselves. We will not feel filled with grudges. We will not spend our lives seeking revenge.

Instead, we will feel that God's love and God's reign are inclusive. No "Susies" are excluded. (Remember the story in the previous chapter where we looked at how Donald Trump attempts to divide us?) Jesus reached out to the poor, to people of other races and ethnicities, to people who were ill or tormented by demons, to people like tax collectors who were considered traitors. We know that every person is a child of God. Every person bears Christ's stamp. We try to love everyone in our lives, and we support efforts by our government and by churches and nonprofits to help people who are suffering.

The Mindset of Ministry

Like Jesus, we will know that we are sent on a mission, empowered by the Holy Spirit or the Spirit of Christ. "As the Father sent me, so I am sending you," the resurrected Christ tells his disciples as he breathes on them and gives them the Holy Spirit. And the purpose of our mission is the same as Jesus' mission – to give birth to the Kingdom of Heaven. Each one of us is unique and as Paul says in 2 Corinthians 12, each of us is endowed with different spiritual gifts. So each one of us will do different things and bring a sense of character that is uniquely ours. But our purpose is to work together to create a world of love and justice that is in balance with the will of God. God created our world and pronounced it good. Our ministry and mission is to create the balance that God intends. We do it proactively. We wake up each morning thinking, "What can I do today to make the world around me a more loving place?"

Power

There is power over other people. Power to dominate them and force them to do what we want. Power to use them to accomplish our goals. Power to make money from their labor. Jesus never exercised this kind of power at all, and neither will we if we are walking his narrow road.

Instead, Jesus embodied the power of God's love to change people's hearts and lives. Jesus used his immense power to be a living demonstration of God's love. Jesus gathered his followers into a loving family who supported each other. Sometimes his disciples and followers squabbled, or thought they should be greater than others, or worried about whether God's love could keep them safe. But time and again, his loving power was more than sufficient, even at the point of his death. When we enter eternal life in the present, we are supported every minute by the presence and power of Christ's Spirit of Love.

By the way, this power that Christ's Spirit gives us is the opposite of what Donald Trump wants us to feel. Donald Trump wants us to believe that we are victims! Just like he always portrays himself as a victim. If you are white, he wants you to feel that you are being replaced by black and brown people who get more advantages than you. If you are male, he wants you to feel that women are taking over your place in the world – which is why he is removing them from leadership in the military and often in the federal government. If you are a native-born citizen, he wants you to feel that your job opportunities are being taken by illegal immigrants who are criminals. If you are straight, he wants you to feel that gay and transgendered people are going to steal the institutions like marriage or sports that preserve your proper place in society.

If Christ's Spirit of Love is empowering your life, then you know already that you are not a victim but a minister. Every person has basic needs, including you, but our needs do not need to splinter us. We can solve all our needs better by working together in love – not by tearing each other down! There is an old preacher's illustration of the difference between heaven and hell. In both heaven and hell, elegant and delicious meals are served at long tables with long silverware – so long that no one can get a piece of food on their fork and get it into their mouths. In hell all the people go hungry, and each meal is torture. In heaven, every meal is a feast, and everyone leaves the table satisfied. The difference? In heaven the people feed each other!

Community

Jesus was a living message to his Jewish brothers and sisters as well as to the whole world that people can live together in peace. His teachings were focused on creating peace. "Treat others as you want them to treat you." ... Forgive not seven times, but seventy-seven!" ... "Be a good neighbor, even to people who are from a different group than you are from (Parable of the Good Samaritan)."

As we look at the history of the church, we see that Christ's Spirit creates community. In Acts 4:32-35 NIV we read about the early church: "All the believers were one in heart and mind. No one claimed that any of their possessions was their own, but they shared everything they had. With great power the apostles continued to testify to the resurrection of the Lord Jesus. And God's grace was so powerfully at work in them all that there were no needy persons among them. For from time to time those who owned land or houses sold them, brought the money from the sales and put it at the apostles' feet, and it was distributed to anyone who had need."

In John 13:35 NIV Jesus says to his followers: "By this everyone will know that you are my disciples, if you have love for one another." If we are experiencing eternal life in the present, we will be in community with others and we will do our part to create and strengthen community.

These are some of the main Biblical signs that we have stepped from the world of the dead into the world of the living. They show us what it means to be a citizen of heaven and yet still be living in this world. In the next chapter we will explore how life feels if we are on the road that leads to darkness and hell.

Reflection Questions

1. Reflect on Jesus' words to us about stepping from the world of the dead to the world of the living: "Anyone here who believes what I am saying right now and aligns himself with the Father, who has in fact put me in charge, has at this very moment the real, lasting life and is no longer condemned to be an outsider." How does this make you feel? In your heart, do you resonate with Jesus' words and feel that your life is aligned with them?

2. In the part of the chapter where we explored Paul's words about having the same mindset as Christ, do you see yourself as a servant of God, sent on a mission to bring Christ's light to the world and thereby help the Kingdom of Heaven to be born? If so, please write some examples of how you do this.

3. Do you understand the difference and the relationship between your executive ego and your Inner Christ? Do you feel that your ego is open to listening to the guidance of your Inner Christ? Do you feel the power of Christ's Spirit at work in you?

4. Take time to listen for the tugging of Christ's Spirit on you as you reflect on the five biblical signs that you are experiencing eternal life in the here and now. What does Christ's Spirit say to you about:
     ◦ Being Centered and Secured by Christ
     ◦ Loving
     ◦ Having the Mindset of Ministry
     ◦ Power
     ◦ Community

8

The Road to Hell

To understand the marks of being on the broad and easy road that leads to destruction, we will take time to consider them in four different but related ways.

The first and most obvious way is to think of the opposites of the five biblical signs which we just saw are signs that we have stepped into eternal life. In each case, we are centered and guided by the living Spirit of Christ. It is our Inner Christ which makes us feel secure and which directs us to create Christ's love in all the dimensions of our lives. So like Christ, we become God's servants. And this is as it should be. As we have seen repeatedly in the scriptures we examined together, it is God's will that we take our marching orders from God. God does not take marching orders from us.

The second way that we will understand why we might be on the tempting road that leads to destruction is to dive into the reason why we might not be centered and guided by our Inner Christ and Christ's powerful Spirit. Here, we will look carefully at the story of Adam and Eve to learn about the conditions of sin (or separation from God) that we all experience in life and that create a basic insecurity that can get the best of us.

Third, having considered Adam and Eve, we will take up Jesus' Sermon on the Mount to see what he says there about receiving our security from God and we will learn from a reflection by Presbyterian minister, Frederick Buechner about the best way to choose a vocation.

Then fourth, we will look together at the Beatitudes to see why it is that Jesus calls things blessed, that we might run away from as things that feel cursed.

All of this taken together will help us understand the forces that might lead us into an easy-looking path that turns out to be the road to destruction.

The opposites of the Signs That We Have Stepped into Eternal Life

A simple way of seeing what we will feel if we are on the highway to hell is to simply take the five biblical signs that we have stepped into eternal life and look for their opposites.

So, if we are on the broad, easy road that leads to destruction we will not feel centered and secured by the living Spirit of Christ, but we will be driven by our executive egos to create our security for ourselves.

We will not start each day with the desire to love every person we meet and to create more love in our world. Instead, we will start by focusing on those we see as our enemies, trying to scheme how to beat them down and control them, or we will start the day lusting for what we don't have enough of and trying to get more of it – money, sex, power over competitors, better clothes, a fancier car, whatever we think might shore up our position in life.

Instead of a mindset of ministry where we look for the guidance of Christ's Spirit and use our personal gifts to be Christ's servant, aiming to create more love and balance in our world, we will have a mindset of personal success, striving to increase our position in our company, our extended family, the city or town we live in, etc.

Instead of feeling that we are moving with the immense power of Christ's Spirit to create love and the deep bonds of community, we will be driven by a self-centered desire to always be in control, to make moves that benefit us. In this, we may very well think we are a victim of someone else's desire to keep us down – and it is possible this is true. There may be anxious, selfish people who are seeking to control us! But if we are moving with Christ's Spirit, we see that we have spiritual gifts and the creative power of love pushing us forward. We know better than to sink to the level of hating an oppressor and we know better than to doubt that God knows how to use us in ministry.

And finally, instead of seeing the power of people to join in Christ's Spirit and work together to create communities of love and justice, we will often try to divide and conquer. This could be inside a family system where we use gossip or a small lie to move another member to get on our side. Or it could be a move inside a business to make us look good and others look bad. Or in Donald Trump's world it could be arming a force like ICE to go into communities and create havoc by arresting migrant workers in a Mexican restaurant or even -- as he has done -- hundreds of workers at a South Korean factory.

At this point you can see the contrast clearly. Jesus always uses love and the eternal power of God's Spirit to minister to the world. His goal is to birth the Kingdom of Heaven on earth where the love and justice that the prophets before him preached become a reality, and the bonds of community bind people of all kinds together in love. Someone who chooses the broad and easy path that leads to destruction is looking out for themselves and a relatively small group of family members or followers to gain control that will give them the things they want at the expense of others. They see life as a zero-sum game. "For me to have more – someone else must have less." So, it is always a competition and a matter of gaining the upper hand and having power over others. Again, this is the way that Donald Trump operates in the world and if you support him, you are not on the narrow path that Jesus says leads to life.

The Human Condition

Our second way of understanding the easy road that leads to destruction is to think carefully about a key story in the Bible. This is the story of Adam and Eve, which reveals the human condition in which we all live. Here we learn why trusting our executive egos to create our security is such a powerful temptation for us.

In the Bible, the great story about what it means to be human is the story of Adam and Eve in the Garden of Eden. This is the second creation story, found in Genesis 2:4-3:24. In this story God forms Adam's body out of the dust of the earth and then breathes life into him by blowing God's breath into Adam's nostrils. God plants a garden bounded by four rivers, sets Adam in the middle of it to till it and keep it, and causes all kinds of trees to grow which become Adam's food. God then sees that it is not good for Adam to be alone, so God begins to create all kinds of animals, bringing each of them to Adam and allowing Adam to name them. In this way, God and Adam form a team, bonding over the wild diversity of life, God creating and Adam naming. In the end, however, God sees that none of the animals is a true partner for Adam, so God causes Adam to fall into a deep sleep. Then God takes one of Adam's ribs and from it forms a companion for him. Adam names her woman for "out of man she is made." At last Adam has a partner and mate.

To this point in the story all is innocence. Adam sees God face to face and glories in God's creative powers. Time is endless. Adam's source of food is limitless. To be sure, Adam is responsible to keep the Garden. However, nothing is created without his knowing and his place of naming each animal gives him knowledge of it. He has no fear. He rejoices in receiving a true partner from God. All is well. Adam feels no doubt, no conflict, no sadness, no loneliness.

If you know the story, however, you know that things are about to change. For a time, things go along beautifully. Adam and Eve like each other and God. They have basic trust in one another. They feel no sense of separation. They move in harmony as partners in a loving family, The only thing Adam and Eve don't understand is God's instruction that they can eat the fruit of any tree in the Garden, but not the fruit of the tree of the knowledge of good and evil. Like small children in the care of a loving and protective parent, they don't know that doing some things can turn out to be dangerous. They have never experienced hurt. They have been held safe by God. "Good" and "evil" are words they don't understand. But they are about to learn.

The serpent – whom Adam has named – is more crafty than any other creature in the Garden. One day he slithers up to Eve and says, "Is it true that you are not allowed to eat the fruit of *any* of the trees in the Garden?" "No," Eve replies. "We can eat all of them except that tree in the middle. On the day we eat that fruit we will die." "Nonsense," says the serpent. "You will not die. God told you that because God knows that when you eat that fruit you will become just like God. You, too, will know the difference between good and evil." Hmmm, Eve thinks. The fruit looks beautiful and nutritious... and if I eat it, I will become wise... so... why not try it... Yes! It's very good. Then she gives some to Adam and he tries it too. But then the eyes of both are opened and they see that they are naked. Suddenly they feel vulnerable in a way they have never felt before. Then they stitch together loincloths out of fig leaves and cover themselves. And they hide from God in the other trees of the Garden.

In eating the fruit, Adam and Eve rebel against God's instruction. They choose a different identity than the initial one that they are given. They exercise free will. What we can learn from this is that we are like them – we have a basic choice between trusting God and choosing to go our own way.

What does it mean for their eyes to be opened? They become self-conscious. Prior to this moment they live in harmony with God and the rest of the Garden. Until the serpent tells Eve that God doesn't want her to become an equal – in fact, wants to keep her inferior -- Eve has no doubt about the order of things. She doesn't divide the world into what's good for me and what's good for others. She simply lives. As soon as Eve and Adam quit trusting God, the unity of creation breaks into a thousand pieces. Now they see a difference between themselves and all other beings in the Garden. Their nakedness threatens them because it can be exploited by others – even by each other. They become ashamed to be naked because their nakedness reveals weakness. So they immediately protect themselves. They cover themselves and hide.

The next part of their story teaches us even more. God comes looking for them and quickly discovers what they have done. There follows a very human scene in which Adam blames his mate (and God who made her and gave her to him) for his eating the forbidden fruit. Eve then blames the serpent (and God who made the serpent) for her disobedience. God is not impressed and cannot give them a second chance, God sees that their change is irreversible and acts accordingly. They can no longer live within the harmony of the Garden, so God casts them out. God does not abandon them, but fashions clothes for them and continues to watch over them. Yet not as before. Never again will they see God face to face, walking in the Garden in the cool of the evening.

Before they leave, God announces to both Adam and Eve what life will be like on the outside. These consequences of their disobedience symbolize the conditions of separation from God that we all must face if life. God tells Eve that her desire will be for her husband, but that Adam will rule over her. God also says that Eve will bear children, but that it will be very painful. God tells Adam that he will now have to work for food and that it will often be difficult. Last, God tells Adam that one day he will die: "I made you from dust; to dust you will one day return."

In the Bible as a whole, the word "sin" means living in a state of separation from God. So the story of Adam and Eve illuminates what sin means. Sin does not primarily refer to the many individual bad things that we humans often do: cheat on our taxes, lie to each other, steal, kill, etc. Rather sin means the fundamental condition of separation from God which we all experience just by being human.

This separation begins when Adam and Eve's eyes are opened into self-consciousness. For better or worse, they see themselves as individuals separate from every other being or thing in the world. How they act on this information will be up to them, but they are always aware of that fundamental divide that Eve first realizes when the serpent suggests to her that there is a difference between what is good for her and what is good for God and she understands the serpent's meaning.

Second, in addition to seeing their separateness, they become profoundly aware of the threats to their existence that God announces to them before they leave the Garden. These threats become known to us, too, as we grow from being very small children who are protected by our parents into older children who can understand the threats of running into the street and being hit by a car, or touching a hot iron. As we get older still, the conditions Adam and Eve face as they live outside the garden come to summarize exactly the things that we most fear.

Like Eve, we all struggle with injustice, even in our most personal relationships. God tells Eve that she will love Adam, yet Adam will rule over her. Rather than being her true partner, Adam will make her serve him and take advantage of her. Please note that this is not what God originally intended for her or wants for any of us. Husbands ruling over wives is not a virtue, but a product of separation from God! Struggle in human relationships and trying to deal with injustice is something that we all experience – women and men both. In the extreme it can be a slave master or an abusive parent or spouse, or a human trafficker. More commonly it will be a cruel boss, a neglectful parent, a cheating business partner, a school bully, or someone who discriminates against us because of our color, ethnicity, sex, sexual orientation, age, etc. The possibilities are endless. We do not live very long without being challenged by injustice in human relationships.

Like Eve, we all experience physical pain. God tells her that she will bear children, yet her labor will be painful. But it is not just women who experience pain. We are all subject to illnesses, accidents, and injuries. Some are small and we quickly recover. But some are excruciating and lead us into torment or even cause us to die.

Like Adam we all work to earn a living under conditions of nature and of society that can destroy our efforts and cause us to fail. It may be farming when a terrible drought develops and there is no water for the crops. It may be owning a business when a depression strikes. It may be losing our means of making a living to the development of some new technology. Even if we grow up extraordinarily wealthy, there is still the possibility that the plane we are taking will crash.

Finally, like Adam, we all will die one day. Under normal circumstances, we learn this by living through the deaths of our grandparents and parents. We miss them when they die. We wonder what has happened to them. We don't like to think of it, but we inevitably wonder and worry about what will happen when we die. Will we just cease to exist? Will the consciousness that is second nature to us suddenly go black?

Because of all of this, life is scary. We are self-conscious. We know that there is no way for us to avoid injustice, pain, and accidents of nature or bad events in society. And no one else can die our death. Inevitably life means struggle in human relationships, suffering physical and emotional pain, working in the face of difficulties, and having our earthly lives come to a permanent end. All this is hard enough. Yet perhaps the worst part is that God, the one power who can truly help us with every one of our fears, is only mysteriously present to us. Like Adam and Eve, we don't ordinarily see God face to face walking in the Garden. We want to receive God's help to relieve our fears, but often we wonder where God is.

Many times, the facts of living under the conditions of sin don't dawn immediately in life. If we are lucky enough to be protected by a loving family, they dawn rather slowly. Yet once they make themselves known, they force us to search for the best answer to the question, "What will make me secure?" As author Jack Kerouac asks, how can we face the fact of our body's eventual disintegration and death and not live in fear?

Trying to Make Ourselves Secure

As we see, life is scary. As we grow and discover just how scary it is, we have a natural desire to become secure. We want to stave off other humans controlling us for their benefit. We want to protect ourselves against diseases and the painful results of accidents. We want to find a way to make a living that secures our income and doesn't expose us to the unpredictable turns of nature or society that ruin crops or cause an economic depression. And we want to live as long as possible.

Under these scary conditions one very human response is to take matters into our own hands and try to make ourselves secure. And as we have seen, as we grow and form our personalities, one thing that naturally happens is that each of us develops what psychologists call an "executive ego." This is the part of us we usually mean when we use the word "I." This is the part that plans our days, figures out what we can do to provide for all the needs we experience, and directs the actions we take to make our lives as secure as possible. So, as we begin to reach our teen years, we start thinking about "what do I want to do when I grow up?" Do I want to go to college, or go into the military, or learn a trade, or join a neighborhood gang and sell drugs, or work on my family's farm, or become a tech designer, or go into modeling, or sing in a rock band, or... There are many possibilities. Most of us end up choosing a path and trying to move forward with it. If we succeed and can make money doing it, we are likely to try harder. If we fail and must rethink our plans, we may fall into a state of depression or hopelessness.

The point to see here is that all this planning and acting is something we may very well do ourselves -- apart from God. We might even say to ourselves, "if I am succeeding, then this must be something God approves of, otherwise God would make me fail." But that turns out to be a bad way of moving with God's Spirit! Recall the so-called "Puritan work ethic." The Puritans immigrated to America in the 1600's and set up colonies. They largely followed Swiss minister and theologian, John Calvin, in believing in predestination – the idea that God had preordained who was going to go to heaven and who was going to hell. Then they wondered, "Well, how can I know if God has preordained me to go to heaven?" And their answer became, "If you are prospering in this life, then it is a sign that God has good things in store for you when you die." But this had the unconscious effect of making the Puritans work harder to prosper in this life and reassure themselves that God had preordained them to go to heaven. Then they started to enjoy being wealthy and the effect of becoming rather rich in comparison to others became an end in itself. So, what started as a sort of spiritual quest became a predominant goal that had nothing to do with God. Puritans began by feeling anxious about their eternal destiny but ended up wanting to be rich because it solved many of the problems of life's insecurities and it was nice to own whatever you needed. This resulted in creating some very selfish people who didn't think of God at all. Dicken's character, Ebenezer Scrooge, the miserable businessman in *A Christmas Carol* is an example of a man who cares only for himself. Thankfully, that story has a happy ending. Scrooge learns the value of kindness and Tiny Tim is saved.

However, human beings' ability to rationalize and excuse what they are doing has produced all kinds of evil in this world that has not ended happily. And, like the Puritans, a lot of that evil has been covered up by religiosity. Here are two examples.

In human history, Christians have rationalized that slavery is ordained by God. In American history, white families that considered themselves Christian took their children to public lynchings of black people where there was a festival atmosphere, and vendors sold food and drinks. This began in 1877 at the end of the Reconstruction period following the Civil War, peaked from1890-1920, and continued into the early 1950s.

In Germany following World War I, Christians got behind Hitler's rise to power and the extermination of Jewish people and many others. Paul Althaus, a prominent Lutheran theologian, wrote in 1933 that Hitler's rise was, "a gift and miracle of God." The German Christians Movement, a pressure group within the German Evangelical Church, aligned itself with the antisemitic, racist, and exalted leadership principles of Nazism and sought to create a "nazified" version of Christianity and a "Reich Church."

There is a very dark side to our response to the insecurities of life and Christians are not exempt. We may well ask, what were the parents thinking who took their children to lynchings? Did they have any sense that eliminating even the semblance of due process was wrong? Did they think that God excuses torture and murder when the people who commit it feel entitled because it will terrorize a group they fear? Did they think the experience was building racial values in their children which they wanted to become strong? Did they have any sense that their actions might be divinely judged and found worthy of eternal condemnation?

It does not seem like the parents were thinking, as much as they were being swept along by public sentiment. It feels like they were carried away by the times, their underlying fear of their former slaves, and their resentment at losing the Civil War.

Having now considered what the story of Adam and Eve teaches us about the human condition, let us go on to look at Jesus' Sermon on the Mount and see what he thinks about the choice we all face, which is do I trust God to be the Source of my security or do I try to make my security for myself?

Jesus' Sermon on the Mount and the Road to Hell

In the Sermon on the Mount, Matthew 7:13-14, Jesus teaches: "You can enter God's Kingdom only through the narrow gate. The highway to hell is broad, and its gate is wide for the many who choose that way. But the gateway to life is very narrow and the road is difficult, and only a few ever find it."

With the insecurity of life and the evil depths that fear creates in us in mind, let's consider the question of what separates those who find the narrow, difficult path to life and those who end up taking the broad, easy highway to hell. What is the critical choice that we make that determines which path we end up taking?

If we look carefully at the rest of Jesus' Sermon on the Mount, we will see again that the choice is between trying to make our security by ourselves, apart from God, or placing a radical trust in God's love and guidance and moving with Christ's Spirit to become ministers of his love. Here are some key examples of this basic choice in the Sermon on the Mount (Matthew 5-7).

Shortly before Jesus' teaching about the narrow gate that leads to life and the broad gate and easy path that leads to destruction, he takes up the subject of God and money. Here is what he says in Matthew 6:19-21, 24-33:

"Don't store up treasures here on earth, where moths eat them and rust destroys them, and where thieves break in and steal. Store your treasures in heaven, where moths and rust cannot destroy, and thieves do not break in and steal. Wherever your treasure is, there the desires of your heart will also be. ...

"No one can serve two masters. For you will hate one and love the other; you will be devoted to one and despise the other. You cannot serve God and be enslaved to money.

"That is why I tell you not to worry about everyday life—whether you have enough food and drink, or enough clothes to wear. Isn't life more than food, and your body more than clothing? Look at the birds. They don't plant or harvest or store food in barns, for your heavenly Father feeds them. And aren't you far more valuable to him than they are? Can all your worries add a single moment to your life?

"And why worry about your clothing? Look at the lilies of the field and how they grow. They don't work or make their clothing, yet Solomon in all his glory was not dressed as beautifully as they are. And if God cares so wonderfully for wildflowers that are here today and thrown into the fire tomorrow, he will certainly care for you. Why do you have so little faith?

"So don't worry about these things, saying, 'What will we eat? What will we drink? What will we wear?' These things dominate the thoughts of unbelievers, but your heavenly Father already knows all your needs. Seek the Kingdom of God above all else, and live righteously, and he will give you everything you need."

When we deal with the insecurity of life by trying to make ourselves secure, money becomes our first concern. Money puts food on the table, a roof over our heads, and clothes on our backs. Unless we want to starve and perhaps watch our children starve, we think we must have enough money. And in American culture right now, money is exalted. The most powerful people are a president who exults in his greed, and tech billionaires who happily purchase his power to open doors so their companies and they can make more billions.

But Jesus knows this way of living pulls us away from God. He says quite directly, no one can worship two masters. We will end up loving only one and hating the other. So it is impossible to love both God and money.

Jesus teaches radical trust. He says that God already knows everything we need and will not hold it back from us. What we must do is to seek God's kingdom first and focus on that. And this is how Jesus, himself, lives. He owns only his sandals and cloak. He travels from place to place preaching and healing. He receives care from the people in the villages he goes to, but he never tries to take advantage of them or to accumulate savings for a rainy day. He is devoted to God and to doing God's works of love.

One of the first things to ask ourselves, then, is how important money and material wealth are to us. If we are on the broad road which leads to destruction, we are likely focused on making ourselves materially successful. We are focused on getting wealthy, and we become anxious and redouble our efforts if things are not going well. It's a matter of what we are paying attention to in life.

Frederick Buechner, a well-known Presbyterian minister and author, writes about finding a vocation in life in his book *Wishful Thinking*. He says:

"Vocation comes from the Latin *vocare*, to call, and means the work a person is called to by God.

"There are all different kinds of voices calling you to all different kinds of work, and the problem is to find out which is the voice of God rather than of Society, say, or the Superego, or Self-Interest.

"By and large a good rule for finding out is this. The kind of work God usually calls you to is the kind of work (a) that you need most to do and (b) that the world most needs to have done. If you really get a kick out of your work, you've presumably met requirement (a), but if your work is writing TV deodorant commercials, the chances are you've missed requirement (b). On the other hand, if your work is being a doctor in a leper colony, you have probably met requirement (b), but if most of the time you're bored and depressed by it, the chances are you have not only bypassed (a) but probably aren't helping your patients much either.

"Neither the hair shirt nor the soft berth will do. The place God calls you to is the place where your deep gladness and the world's deep hunger meet."

Our deep gladness... We live besieged by commercials trying to sell us something, by companies trying to use our phone clicks to learn what we will buy, by dating sites in which prospective dates project beauty and material success. It's as if our main goal in life is to become a successful commodity. But where is our deep gladness? Where do we get to dance with Christ's Spirit to discover and learn to use the spiritual gifts that God gives us? Where do we practice ministry in Buechner's vision of employing our spiritual gifts to meet one of the world's great needs?

There is a soul-satisfying dimension to life that is vulnerable to being squashed in many ways. It can be squashed by extreme poverty to the point where children suffer malnutrition or they grow up in such poverty that they never develop a sense of hope that the larger world holds a good place for them as they become adults. It can be squashed by family abuse or by vicious bullying. It can be squashed by alcohol or drug abuse. It can be squashed by the shallowness of our materialistic society which sends the message that money and power over others are everything.

Yet God gifts all of us. We all have an Inner Christ to guide us in the ways of love. When we move with that Inner Christ and Christ's larger Spirit then we discover vast pools of creative energy within us to form relationships of love and to meet the world's great hunger for resonance with God's values – the original values of the Garden God created for Adam and Eve. In that Garden everything lived in balance. Nothing dominated. Each form of life supported the others. There was harmony and peace. And God was at the center of it all.

Today we are in deep trouble because the direction our government is leading us in is the opposite of the balance and harmony of God's Garden. Instead of unity our government creates division. Instead of love, what is preached is hate. Instead of mutual encouragement there is blame. Instead of a place for everyone, people are being cast out without a semblance of due process. Instead of deep values there are golden toilets. Instead of spirituality there is naked lust and greed. Instead of respecting God's wisdom there is the invasive spying of AI. Instead of respecting and preserving nature there is, "Drill baby, drill!" If we dance to those rhythms we are most definitely on the highway to hell.

Considering the Beatitudes

The final way we will look at this is to think together about the Beatitudes with which Jesus begins his Sermon on the Mount. Like Moses going up to the top of Mt. Sinai and returning with the Ten Commandments, Jesus goes to the top of a mountain to teach how we become blessed. In the first two beatitudes, he makes clear that knowing that we need God is a blessing in itself. We cannot make our own security no matter how hard we try. One point of evidence for this is that 100% of humans physically die. A giant yacht may be a place to hide from COVID, but no matter what we own, we will all die. Knowing we need God is an important key to finding the narrow path that leads to life.

Here is what Jesus teaches:

"God blesses those who are poor and realize their need for God, for the Kingdom of Heaven is theirs."

Dr. Richard W. Swanson writes that another translation of this can be, "God blesses those whose breath has been stolen and who realize their need for Spirit." The NIV translation of this beatitude is: "Blessed are the poor in spirit, for theirs is the kingdom of heaven." But to be poor in spirit can be translated as being "breath-less." The behavior of our federal government is stealing the breath of the people. It is stealing the Spirit we need for life away from us. Hence, in our gasping for the Source of real life we know our need for God, the creator of spiritual breath.

"God blesses those who mourn, for they will be comforted."

We often take this to mean we are blessed when we mourn the loss of a loved one and God will comfort us. But we mourn for many things – including the direction of our national life. And God will comfort us in this need as well.

"God blesses those who are humble, for they will inherit the whole earth.

Those who are humble do not try to take the place of God in creating their own security. They know their limits, and they are content to place themselves in God's hands.

"God blesses those who hunger and thirst for justice, for they will be satisfied.

Because of the movement of God's Spirit, doing justice begets more justice. Those who work for justice will see it born and nurtured.

"God blesses those who are merciful, for they will be shown mercy.

Because of the movement of God's Spirit, showing mercy begets more mercy.

"God blesses those whose hearts are pure, for they will see God.

When our hearts are pure and unobstructed by fear, greed, selfishness, and anger, then we can see God's face in the face of Christ and dance with Christ's Spirit.

"God blesses those who work for peace, for they will be called the children of God.

When we work for the total shalom (or complete peace) that God intends for creation, we step into the destiny that God has created for us from the beginning of time.

"God blesses those who are persecuted for doing right, for the Kingdom of Heaven is theirs.

When we are persecuted for working for justice, we enter the Kingdom of Heaven in the here and now because we have followed Jesus' teaching. Remember what he says later in Matthew? "If any of you wants to be my follower, you must give up your own way, take up your cross, and follow me. If you try to hang on to your life, you will lose it. But if you give up your life for my sake, you will save it. And what do you benefit if you gain the whole world but lose your own soul? Is anything worth more than your soul? For the Son of Man will come with his angels in the glory of his Father and will judge all people according to their deeds." Matthew 16:24-27

So from the Beatitudes, the qualities that lead to eternal life are:

- Mourning the loss of a person or a quality of life
- Knowing your need for God by being poor in spirit
- Being humble
- Desiring and working for justice
- Offering mercy
- Keeping a pure heart
- Creating peace; and
- Being persecuted for working for justice

Conversely, the opposite qualities that almost certainly lead to the highway to hell are:

- Trying to get everything you need by yourself
- Ignoring the pain of living and the pain of the world around you
- Being puffed up thinking you are better and more deserving than others
- Ignoring justice in favor of working for the deal that helps you best
- Hardheartedness, holding grudges

- Lusting for what others have that you want (sex, possessions, power)
- Creating conflicts or even wars
- Getting away with doing injustice

Again, an even briefer way of summarizing the difference is to say that the qualities that lead to eternal life are the ones that recognize that God is the center and we are God's servants... while the qualities that lead to hell and destruction are the ones that put us at the center, beholding to no one.

What About Evangelical Churches That Support Donald Trump?

All this said, it is easy to imagine church members actively involved in a church that supports Donald Trump, but that also in many genuine ways supports them. Inside that church there may truly be many opportunities to serve the loving values of Christ and to move with his Spirit. The church may have small groups where members gather for fellowship and can bear their souls talking about the problems of everyday life. Members in the group truly care for each other. When one member has a problem, others come to their aid. This is genuine Christian love. Moreover, the church may hold exciting worship services, have a dynamic worship leader, and have inspiring music. There may be programs for children and youth. The church may have a pantry for the wider community, and it may have various kinds of outreach to help children struggling in school or to help improve the cleanliness and beauty of poor neighborhoods. In the church, leaders may believe that their support of Donald Trump is helping build a Christian nation and that his leadership will protect the nation from evil influences coming from the left of the political spectrum.

Isn't this good, then? Does belonging to this church place their members' souls in jeopardy?

Life isn't always simple, and we can feel two very different things at the same time. Asking this question about such a church might be compared to asking how belonging to a crime family might turn out for the members. The Sopranos television series follows the life of a mob boss named Tony Soprano who begins secretly seeing a therapist after he suffers a panic attack. As the series unfolds, the stress on Tony of growing up in a very dysfunctional family is revealed. Now as he rises to power, he has difficulty juggling the requirements of his criminal life with the needs of his family. He and the family members often draw our sympathy because we identify with their human struggles. But the fact remains that his life is not built on a solid foundation and that extremely violent and harmful things are done.

As we have seen many times, Donald Trump and his administration have done extremely harmful things and are trying to turn the United States from a democracy into a kind of theocratic dictatorship – one that grossly favors the rich and uses the poor. This corrupt foundation eventually corrupts everything that gets close to it – including churches that may see Donald Trump as some kind of instrument of God. The domination and power over all others that he seeks cannot help but have ruinous effects on everything that gets close to him. Churches that do not recognize this and do not resist – in loving and nonviolent ways! – are churches that are building on the same foundation and will come to ruin to the detriment of their members. We saw it in Nazi Germany, and it can certainly happen here.

Reflection Questions

1. The story of Adam and Eve ends up showing us that life is scary and that almost without realizing it, we are likely to try to create our own security without trusting God and intentionally moving with God's Spirit. As you think about your life, how are you choosing to try to become secure?

2. Many times in the Gospels Jesus teaches or tells parables about the way that loving money destroys our faith in God. Do you see examples of how his teachings ring true as we look into the behavior of the Trump administration?

3. Are there certain Beatitudes which you feel express deep ways that you are connected with God and Jesus? Are there some which make you wonder why Jesus said them?

4. How do you feel about Frederick Buechner's definition of vocation as the place where your deep gladness and the world's deep hunger meet? Do you feel that you have a vocation that you practice? If so, how does it help you move with Christ's Spirit?

5. Do you agree that looking at the Beatitudes and their opposites helps us know the difference between being on the narrow path that leads to experiencing eternal life now – and being on the broad highway that leads to destruction? If you agree, how do you feel? If you don't agree, what would be a better way to compare the two?

6. Overall, how do you assess your life right now? Are you on the narrow path where you are already experiencing eternal life in the present? Or are you on the broad road that leads to destruction?

9

Changing Hearts and Minds

First, if you have made it this far, thank you very much for taking time to consider this eternally important issue of God's expectations for us and of the day of judgment that the Bible says every person will one day face. Our human lives here on earth are not even the blink of an eye compared to eternity, so for us, individually, there can be no other issue as important as this one.

Second, if you have been supporting Donald Trump or are a pastor or leader of a church that supports him, then you have come to a fork in the road. Will you choose the narrow path that leads to life – or will you remain on the broad path that, according to every Bible passage that we have examined, leads to destruction?

A very familiar Bible story may help us here – the story of Zacchaeus the tax collector. Let's read it from Luke 19:1-10:

Jesus entered Jericho and made his way through the town. There was a man there named Zacchaeus. He was the chief tax collector in the region, and he had become very rich. He tried to get a look at Jesus, but he was too short to see over the crowd. So he ran ahead and climbed a sycamore-fig tree beside the road, for Jesus was going to pass that way.

When Jesus came by, he looked up at Zacchaeus and called him by name. "Zacchaeus!" he said. "Quick, come down! I must be a guest in your home today."

Zacchaeus quickly climbed down and took Jesus to his house in great excitement and joy. But the people were displeased. "He has gone to be the guest of a notorious sinner," they grumbled.

Meanwhile, Zacchaeus stood before the Lord and said, "I will give half my wealth to the poor, Lord, and if I have cheated people on their taxes, I will give them back four times as much!"

Jesus responded, "Salvation has come to this home today, for this man has shown himself to be a true son of Abraham. For the Son of Man came to seek and save those who are lost."

The setting for this story is that Jesus and his disciples are on the way to Jerusalem where Jesus will be crucified during the festival of Passover. They reach Jericho, not far from Jerusalem, and crowds are abuzz with the news that Jesus – teacher and healer – is here.

Zacchaeus is a Jewish tax collector, the chief tax collector in fact, and he has become very rich. Yet he is collecting taxes on behalf of the occupying force in Israel, the Romans, and he has become a hated traitor to his own people. Something in Zacchaeus is stirred by the news that Jesus is in his city. He must have heard of Jesus and something about what he has heard tugs on his heart. To put it into the psychological terms we used earlier, although Zacchaeus' executive ego has plotted out this way for him to become rich, his soul – or his inner Christ – nevertheless knows that he is wildly out of balance with God's will. So Zacchaeus wants to see for himself what Jesus looks like. Yet when he gets out on the street, he is short of stature and can't see Jesus because too many people are blocking his sight. So amazingly, he runs ahead and climbs a sycamore tree! As Jesus comes near, Jesus spies him and takes initiative. "Zacchaeus!" Jesus calls, "Come right down for I must stay at your house today!" No one is expecting this. The crowd can't believe that Jesus wants anything to do with a sinner like Zacchaeus. Zacchaeus can't either, but he is delighted. He scrambles down and brings Jesus to his home. Then unbidden, Zacchaeus does the right thing – something that Jesus proclaims brings salvation to his house. "I will give half my wealth to the poor, Lord, and if I have cheated people on their taxes, I will give them back four times as much!"

Caught up in the compassion of Jesus, Zacchaeus reforms himself. He makes what seems an incredible promise to the onlookers. And Jesus believes him, says that salvation has now come to his house, and then points to Zacchaeus as an example of what he has been sent by God to do: to seek and to save the lost.

Now, caught up in the compassion of Jesus, supporters of the Trump administration who feel the leading of their souls, can do the same thing: turn away from their previous path and begin to fix the harm that path has caused. Zacchaeus proclaimed to Jesus and to the crowd what he was doing. He made it public. And then he followed through.

Since 2012, I have worked with clergy and community leaders to create and grow a gang and youth violence intervention program in Buffalo, NY called the Buffalo Peacemakers. Working cooperatively with the Buffalo Police Department and other community groups we have played a major role in reducing shootings and other assaults by teenagers and young adults. We also run a safe passage program to help young people get to school and return home safely each school day, and we run a unique mentoring program for about 80 justice-involved youth per year, ages 14-20.

The reason for bringing up the Buffalo Peacemakers is that nearly all our adult mentors were themselves in trouble with the law when they were growing up and the majority served time in prison. Yet in each mentor's life, there came a time when they repented – that is, they realized that the path they were on was a path that led to destruction. At the same time, they also felt the call of Christ to join him and begin to do the same acts of healing love that he did. So they changed their hearts and minds! They gave up doing harmful things and began to intentionally repair the damage they had done. This kind of powerful change is possible and perhaps is an example of what Jesus meant when he said, "There is more joy in heaven over one lost sinner who repents and returns to God than over ninety-nine others who are righteous and haven't strayed away!" (Luke 15:7) In our experience in Buffalo, the thing troubled youth tell us again and again is, "No one listens to me!" But these mentors meet our youth at least five days a week. They use restorative circles to build listening skills. They take time to listen one-on-one. The program runs all year. Each youth builds a relationship with at least one stable, experienced mentor who has experienced and survived the same stressful conditions they are facing, and who takes time to listen to them carefully and to respond compassionately.

Now you can take the path Zacchaeus took. You can take the path our Peacemakers mentors took. You may already feel that you love Jesus. And because life is complicated, you may already be treating many people in the loving ways Christ teaches us to treat others. Yet if you and your church support the Trump administration and its many harmful policies and actions, then you are greatly out of step with the ministry of Jesus! I am sorry that is true. But when you review how Jesus actually lived and the biblical teachings he taught, you can clearly see that this is true.

For your own sake, and for the welfare of so many others including children in your community and across the world, please change direction. Get off the broad, easy road that moves down a supposedly pious but actually harmful way that so many evangelicals and Trump supporters have chosen to take. Instead, get onto that narrow but extraordinarily loving path your inner Christ is calling you to take. Give yourself fully to use your unique spiritual gifts to make our nation and world more loving and less divisive. Support and work for policies that help children and families prosper, especially those who are challenged by poverty, poor health, homelessness, or discrimination. Reject and separate yourself from the authoritarian, lying, fear-mongering ways of the Trump administration that benefit billionaires and leave middle-class and poor people in the lurch. Talk with your family members and church members and leaders about why you are changing and why they should soulfully consider changing, too.

If you read the gospel stories about Jesus and then pray for his Spirit to enfold your heart, you will soon move away from following the un-thinking crowd that claims to be Christian while supporting the division and oppression of Donald Trump and his administration. Then you can become a true citizen of heaven even as you live in this world. Then you can truly offer Christ's compassion and love to those who are most in need.

Let the Jesus we meet on the pages of the New Testament and the Jesus who resides in your heart be your guide. I pray that it will be so for you.

Reflection Questions

1. Knowing what the Bible says about judgment, do you want to be judged holding hands with Donald Trump as a supporter of how he has acted as president?

2. Knowing what you have reviewed about Jesus' life and teachings about loving your enemies, caring for the poor, the importance of children, welcoming and caring for foreigners in your midst, and creating a community of love -- do you want to be remembered by your family as someone driven by hate, bitterness, a desire to create division, a sense of always being persecuted by others, and a huge greed for money?

While the author is responsible for what is ultimately written, I wish to thank many people who read the manuscript as it developed and helped greatly. These include my editor, Conrad Kanagy, an authors' group associated with Santos Publishing, and a professional Practice of Ministry group in Western New York. That group not only read the manuscript cover to cover but met with me twice in person for detailed discussions. The members of that group are Rev. Dr. Theodore Brelsford, Rev. Gary Gossel, Rev. Paula Gustafson, Rev. Laurie Heidenreich, Rev. Dr. M. Bruce McKay, Rev. Dr. Ruth Snyder, and Rev. Dale Stanley. I deeply appreciate all the help and encouragement I received.

Rev. Dan Schifeling

www.ingramcontent.com/pod-product-compliance
Lightning Source LLC
Chambersburg PA
CBHW071439130726
47997CB00006B/2155